THE VERBALS

IAIN SINCLAIR

in conversation with

KEVIN JACKSON

THE VERBALS

worple press

First published 2003 by
Worple Press
12 Havelock Road
Tonbridge
Kent TN9 1JE

ISBN 0-9539479-0

Worple Press is an independent publisher specialising in poetry,
art and alternative titles. **Worple Press** can be contacted at:

PO Box 238, Tonbridge, Kent TN9 1WR
Email: theworpleco@aol.com
Fax: 01732 368 958

Typeset and printed by Peepal Tree Press, Leeds

CONTENTS

In Memoriam

Stan Brakhage, film-maker
&
Roy Porter, historian

'Nonulli perierunt in opere nostro'

I.S. and K.J.

DOING THE VERBALS

We were first thrown together by the Krays. I was fronting a documentary about twins in art and life for BBC Radio Four - *Comedy of Errors* and *Twelfth Night*, Michel Tournier's *Gemini*, Cronenberg's *Dead Ringers*, that kind of thing - and the producer said that he thought that we needed some kind of major Kray Twins digression. He was already a Sinclair fan, knew about Sinclair's gargantuan fund of recondite East End lore, and duly summoned our author into one of the small, not to say claustrophobia-inducing self-op studios on the seventh floor of Broadcasting House. We sat face to face, Sinclair and I, two bulbous microphones between us. The DAT rolled.

First impressions: big, tall bloke, formidable pate (oversize brain?), alarmingly fit, dauntingly solemn, with a habit of tilting his head forward and looking up enquiringly over his glasses, like a public school headmaster about to go ballistic on a Latin set that has fallen behind on its quotas for deponent verbs. Definitely officer class - if not a posh headmaster, then probably a high-ranking cleric, regional bank manager, or consultant specialising in some exceptionally rare and unpleasant neurological disorder. Then there was the voice: "educated", English (no hint of the Welsh childhood or the Scottish deep roots), quiet, well modulated, sweetly reasonable. Until you listened to the content.

If this were a novel, or a slightly more mendacious memoir, I would now say that his words burned themselves into my brain forever. The truth is that all I can remember is a sudden lurch in topic which began with an unforeseen phrase, something like "and, of course, this is really all about voodoo", and then a lengthy screed about Ron and Reggie disappearing to - was it Nigeria? - and participating in some hideous local rites, some murky conjuring of ancient African gods or spirits. Was Sinclair winding me up? Just kidding? I couldn't tell. (I still can't.) But I was intrigued.

7

A couple of years passed. Sinclair was about to publish something called *Lights Out for the Territory*, and once again the BBC - this time it was Radio Three - made a date for us. I read the advance copy, loved it, found it funny and fascinating and crammed with deliciously, refreshingly arcane matter. A fan was born. Abigail Appleton, the producer, got us to mooch around in the back streets near BH and yammer psychogeography while she danced nimbly around us with a portable tape recorder. I tried to keep my end of the conversation up by throwing in some juicy details about the making of Donald Cammell's *Performance* which I'd turned up in the course of writing a (mercifully, unproduced) screenplay. Naturally, Sinclair had got there first.

Once is happenstance, twice is coincidence, the third time is enemy action. In the summer of 1999, the *Independent* despatched me to walk a section of the M25 route with Sinclair. The rest is literature. You can read Sinclair's account of that day's walking, and of three subsequent M25 treks including the Nightmare of Waltham Abbey, in *London Orbital* (Granta, 2002). Needless to say, the verbal portrait of me which appears in that book is a vile and ill-spirited caricature, much as I'd been expecting. But what the book leaves opaque is my motive for exposing myself to so much needless pedal agony and spiritual humiliation.

One answer is that I liked the talk so much. Couldn't get enough of it. Where else in civilian life do you get the chance to natter and swap yarns uninterruptedly for 10 to 12 hours with such a... how to style our author? A scholar and a gentleman? A magus? A visionary poet? A wit and rancounteur? An obssessive? A bleeding nutter? All of this and more, probably. In those rambles we covered a thousand, thousand topics, and, as far as I recall, never once did I touch on a subject or person or book that Sinclair hadn't met, read, studied or flogged for a quick profit. William Seabrook, once-famous American journalist and dabbler in the occult? Check. Gregory Bateson's *Naven*? Check. John Lilly, the dolphin man and ketamine freak? Check, check and mate.

Even when the M25 epic was done, we kept in touch for fun and profit. I hauled him in for another radio documentary, on William Blake, and for the Blakean *Tygers of Wrath* concert/event/ happening at the Queen Elizabeth Hall, where Sinclair and his long-time oppo Brian Catling shared the stage with the likes of Billy Bragg, Jah Wobble, Alan Moore and a scratch band featuring quondam members of the Sex Pistols and Blur, with rapping from Ewan McGregor. (Sounds like a great evening. Wish I could remember it. Bad calculation of precisely how much red wine was needed to calm the MC's stage fright.) Then Sinclair hauled me in to re-enact some of my pain for the "London Orbital" event at the Barbican. (Sounds like a great evening, even though J.G. Ballard didn't turn up, and had to be replaced by a cardboard cut-out. Wish I could remember it.)

So this book of interviews, *The Verbals*, was probably inevitable: Johnson and Boswell, Goethe and Eckermann, Burke and Hare. Inevitable, anyway, once I had introduced Sinclair to my old mucker Peter Carpenter - poet, publisher, teacher and world's leading expert in the ephemera of Epsom. (Again, see *London Orbital* for the sordid details.) I went down to Sinclair's new bolt-hole by the sea in Hastings for a couple of taping sessions in November 2002 or thereabouts, then topped those interviews up with a visit to his Hackney gaff in early February 2003. Anything was up for grabs, he said, except for family stuff. Fair enough: I decided to make it mainly biographical, and to concentrate on the earlier, less well documented parts of Sinclair's life and career(s), taking it that most of his recent activities were part of the public record. I'm happy to report that the talk held quite a few surprises, even after all our hours on the roads. I mean, take all that stuff about auditory hallucinations in Whitechapel... spooky.

Consider your good fortune, subtle and discriminating reader. Now, you too can experience something of the range and flavour of a full-blown Sinclairian ramble, in the (assumed) comfort of your own home or train seat, and all without blisters or seeping toenails. Respect due to Amanda Carpenter of Worple Press for countless contributions to making this book possible; to Anna Sinclair for putting up with repeated disruptions of domestic life; to Ron and Michele Royal for generously allowing me to stay in the house while writing it all up; and to Iain Sinclair for playing along with the scheme so whole-heartedly. As they say in these parts: "Enjoy!"

KJ
Moosebay, South Bristol, Maine
21 February 2003.

PART ONE:

CHILDHOOD AND SCHOOL

KJ: Let's begin with the Freemasons, as they're obviously behind everything that's happened for the last three hundred years anyway. Is there any truth, as you hint there just might be in *Lights Out for the Territory*, to the story that you're descended from the mysterious St Clair family, the builders of the Rosslyn Chapel?

IS: I really don't know. It's a fabulous fiction that has haunted me since the sixties, about the Sinclair/ St Clair family being hereditary Templars, and the Priory of Zion conspiracy theory comes in on top of this...I think I must have heard about it in the early days of book-hunting, rummaging around street markets. It's almost like the myth about the foundation of the Golden Dawn...

Those fragments are delivered in places like Farringdon Road book market - and at the same time messengers would come up, strange figures in the book markets, and tell stories. People like Joseph Sickert, who initially put up this business that became the story of William Gull, John Netley and Walter Sickert. Surgeon, coachman, painter. And their involvement in a Masonic plot to murder Whitechapel prostitutes. Joseph Sickert claimed to be the illegitimate son of Walter Sickert - there's no very definite proof of this, but he's a character who lived around Islington, where Sickert had his connections. Sickert's papers are in the archive at Islington Library. And Joseph would tell people, for the price of a few drinks, the story that his father was supposed to have pitched - that he had direct knowledge of the Ripper murders.... this scenario involves Sir William Gull cleaning-up the traces of an illegitimate Royal child... that kind of information comes to me directly, or refracted through other people, bits of stuff overheard in pubs, and sometimes leads up to a point where there's a book. At one time I knew

Richard Leigh, who was one of the authors of *The Holy Blood and the Holy Grail*, that group of people. He ran a kind of Anti-University in Notting Hill, or was going to...

KJ: Was that THE anti-University?

IS: No, it wasn't *The* - Anti-University.. I don't know if you can have THE Anti-University [Laughs], or the Anti-University that [R.D.] Laing and Alex Trocchi were doing was in Rivington Street, on the edge of Shoreditch. But Leigh and other people kicked one off in Notting Hill, and I went to talk to him, met him there, and I was going to do a London psychogeography - before the word was up and running - about Hawksmoor churches and mythical alignments and all the rest of it. But this never came about - the brochure was produced but the thing collapsed. But meeting him, I got in on the ground floor of the *Holy Blood* story [about the supposed lineage of Christ and related mysteries] that would become an international best-seller, however preposterous.

KJ: Were you tickled by the idea of this possiblity of a deep background in the Templars?

IS: It's quite good fun. I treat it as a kind of myth, in a perspex box. It played along with other elements in a provocative way.

KJ: To turn to the realms of reality, you do have at least one writer in your family background?

IS: Well, sort of. My great-grandfather, Arthur Sinclair, wrote an account of his life which is about the size of a book of stamps. His style, I found, uncannily, was quite close to my own. [Laughs]. Poor man! Quite jokey, satiric, free-flowing. He says at the beginning of this micro-biography that he came from discounted Jacobite stock, living in a removed country situation, I imagine on some very small farm, pretty impoverished. And he gives an account of going to school, having to walk miles to get there - usual stuff. And then he says, "I left school at 10" (or whatever it was) "and commenced my education" - that sort of tone. He walked into Aberdeen and bought De Quincey... but his main thing was that he became a self-taught naturalist and plantsman. He was patronised by some minor Scottish aristocrat who, in the way they did, shipped him off to Ceylon, where he became on adviser on soil management for tea plantations, and after a long period there, made enough money to retire in style to Scotland and have lots of children.

But then all the money was lost, in some unspecified financial disaster on the market, and he took off and became a seriously strange traveller, to places like the source of the Amazon - wandering about in Peru, and gold-prospecting in Tasmania, and then he began to write, a book about his travels in the Amazon - which I've got - with maps and other details, which I've drawn on from time to time. So he was firstly a botanist and artist - he drew plants as well - and secondly a writer, a semi-professional writer. His books came out from proper presses, but a lot of what he wrote appeared first in newspapers in Ceylon.

KJ: Any other writers in the family?

IS: Not as far as I know. On the Scottish side of the family, no. That's the end of the line - I know the story only as far back as this great-grandfather. His son, my grandfather, was a younger son. He became a doctor, a GP, and came to South Wales, and my father followed him. So that's it on my father's side; on my mother's side, they were Welsh aboriginals...

KJ: What was your mother's maiden name?

IS: Jones. [Laughs] And they came from Cardiganshire and Carmathen and the West of Wales, and were all Welsh-speaking. They did write - they all write Welsh poetry, and they all preached and performed. They were a celtic version of Southern Gothic, *Wise Blood*, *Night of the Hunter*, mad preachers... or teachers, or just farmers, workers in coal-mines. They migrated east to the mining

15

valleys, and my mother was working as a dispensing chemist and doctor's receptionist when she met my father.

KJ: It's very noticeable to anyone who reads your book jacket blurbs that they often begin "Iain Sinclair is the son of a doctor"...

IS: *I* don't say that! That's nothing to do with me. At one point, I think Neil Belton, my editor at Granta Books wanted to make me sound slightly more respectable. [Laughs] Normally, it was this stuff about, "...has worked in parks departments, cigar packer...". And for some reason, I don't know how he found it out, Neil stuffed that on a dust jacket and it's popped up time and again, ever since.

KJ: Well, that explodes everything I'd been planning to ask about filial piety...

IS: None of that at all. Though my father certainly had a sense of wanting to be a writer himself, much in demand as an after-dinner speaker. He was very, very funny and a natural storyteller, with his reminiscences of being a young doctor..., A. J. Cronin routines. He was going to go into tropical medicine, he was very bright, took a top degree at Aberdeen, and his plan in life was to follow the Scottish trajectory out to somewhere hot, uncomfortable and unhealthy. But his own father was taken ill, he came back - he'd qualified as a doctor by the time he was 21 or so, very young - came back temporarily to look after things in Wales, and his father got seriously ill and died, and he never got away. So I think there was a sense of frustration there. And his stories of arrving back in Wales were really Stevensonian. His first call-out was to a remote cottage - this would be in the early 30s - and someone had just cut their throat, and there was blood running down the stairs. Then there were stories about amputations he had to do underground, because he was doctoring the coal mines. I think at the back of his mind he thought, one day I'll retire and I'll write all this material up. But he never did, he just carried on working, on and off, until he died.

KJ: Was he someone you admired?

IS: Oh, yes. Absolutely. I thought that this kind of life, being a GP in this society, was very useful. The hours they worked - I just couldn't believe it. Saturdays, Sundays.. you'd get called out often two or three times a night. Too much for me, I couldn't have contemplated it.

KJ: Doctors' families are quite often dynastic, aren't they? Sons and daughters following fathers and mothers into the profession...

IS: Well, he'd done that, and there was a hovering expectation that this was what I would do, too, but it soon became obvious that it wasn't going to happen, because I had no inclination towards the sciences. And I was also fairly determined in my way to do what I knew I was going to do.

KJ: Does that imply you had a notion of being a writer from a very early age?

IS: Oh yeah, yeah.

KJ: How early is early?

IS: Well, I don't know - fourteen, fifteen... I mean, I knew that was what I was doing, but I didn't have any expectation of being able to make a living from it. That never occurred to me. I just thought, well, I do this, and I'll do something else, it didn't matter too much what, to survive - the more interesting the better, moving across the landscape doing odds and ends, and keep the other side going just as a sort of eccentricity of my own.

KJ: Back to childhood. Again, according to the jacket blurbs, you were born in Cardiff, in 1943?

IS: I was born in Cardiff, but that was somewhat accidental. We didn't live in Cardiff, we lived in a town called Maesteg, an agricultural town that had been overtaken by industry. There were five coal mines all around it, and my mother's father had been an accountant and manager in one of the coal mines. But because my mother had a very difficult first birth - she was very small, only about five foot tall...

KJ: But you're well over six foot; you get your height from your father?

IS: He was taller than me, more the height of my son Will. Anyway, she had a difficult first childbirth, and lost the child, so when she went into labour with me they went to a nursing home in Cardiff rather than the local cottage hospital, in the middle of a major air raid, parts of the docks burning. But I was brought home almost immediately after being born, and spent my childhood in Maesteg, going to an eccentric Dame school. An Irish Catholic woman ran it, and I went there until the age of seven. The Old Testament, inky fingers and blots on a heavy, tasselled tablecloth.

KJ: So, a fairly ordinary rural childhood?

IS: There was a strong sense of the place I lived in, which was a little town, with easy access to the countryside, and only about six miles to the sea, so the sea plays quite a big part - there were lots of expeditions to the sea, and the whole thing occurs in the aftermath of the war. There was a sense that things were threadbare and tight. The first big trip away was up to London to see the Festival of Britain [in 1951]... so the first sense of London was pretty extraordinary - the train to Paddington, and then being out on the river.... going down the river, to Tower Bridge, that landscape lodging in my head from the very start as being somewhere really magical, and the colour and smell of London, the grey-brownness. It seemed to be always wet, as well, which all proved to be true...

KJ: Did you have siblings?

IS: No, there was just my mother's first child, a girl who lived for a few months and then died. After me, that was enough. But I had a lot of friends in the immediate neighbourhood - it was the sort of society where you moved in and out of other people's houses, so I wandered freely up and down this hill. The house next door belonged to a builder who had a large, jungly garden with raspberry bushes and lawns, so I was endlessly backwards and forwards there. There was no sense of being isolated, solitary, in a golden tower.

KJ: And not a place where class distinctions counted for much among the children?

IS: There was a kind of very Welsh, middle-class snobbery which did operate to some extent, but those kind of distinctions didn't really hold on the streets, except that the town was zoned into different groups and gangs - groups of Irish, this and that - and there was a certain amount of brigandry between these groups. But there was great sense of being able to move around in ways that my children certainly couldn't in London.

KJ: You make it sound rather Tom Sawyer-ish - outdoorsy, lots of rough and tumble...

IS: Yes, that was basically it. There were very few intellectual interests. [Laughs]. It was basically being out in a landscape that was interesting, and relatively safe to explore on a local level, and there were all these industrial ghosts - mills, railway lines, pit-props you could build into log cabins. I guess it was already decaying, slightly, but it was all still there. My fascination was with ruins - brick buildings that looked like, I guess I would say now, Mayan temples that had been something industrial, but I don't know what. Almost a Ballardian landscape. And being in a valley, there were mountains or small hills on each side, and the thing was to get to these and climb them. And when you reach the top, the scenery just rolls away - you realise where you are, the hills go away forever, and how far could you go? - and wanting to move across that, and then gradually finding that if you go over this one, there's a conifer plantation, and if you go through that, you see the sea! There it is! And I can remember the first day we cycled to the coast, and realised that this small place that seemed to be the whole world actually opens up to the ocean and...

KJ: I don't want to pursue an Anthony Clare line of questioning too far, but presumably at some time you must have speculated about what it means to you to have a missing older sibling.

IS: Yeah. I think I can remember, as an adolescent, having romantic notions about siblings and ghosts and potential incest, all that, thinking about it. But not really thinking about it since. Not at all. It's never been an obsession... but it *is* there. I mean, there must be some sense of somebody ahead of me, a girl, who is missing but is still a presence.

KJ: Was she ever alluded to in your childhood?

IS: Yes, my mother would talk quite openly about this, and it was obviously a big loss. She was reasonably old when she married, by the standards of the time - in her thirties - so losing the first child put a lot of pressure on the second one who survived. I think my own birth was not at all easy, I was a blue baby, they were worried I wasn't going to take breath, and - this is a family myth -my father came in with this pile of books, dropped one on my head - a novel called *Crackerjack*, a crime novel. I gave a great yell, and that was it, the whole thing was launched.

KJ: Literature saved you...

IS: ...Or pulp fiction. I haven't found the book, but it's in the bibliographies of detective fiction: *Crackerjack*. By W. B. M. Ferguson. Long, 1936

KJ: What next in your education, after you left the village school?

IS: When you get to seven, eight, nine, the decision was, do you go through into the local school system, take the 11-plus, maybe make it to the local grammar school, or else submerge into the educational underclass - middle class neuroses kick in and parents decide the best we can do is to send them off to school somewhere.

KJ: Did that amount to quite a financial sacrifice for your parents?

IS: I think, looking back on it, it must have been very tight, because my father didn't earn a lot as a GP, but then I was an only child and private education wasn't as expensive a business then as it is now, not anything like. I think it was within their compass, but it did take a big chunk of their earnings. So I went away to a Welsh prep school between seven and nine, and then I think they began to think of the next jump ahead, which was to try to get me into a Public School. I went first to a school, not very far away, on the coast in place called Porthcawl... A kind of resort, with a huge caravan park.

KJ: It's in *Landor's Tower*...

IS: It comes into the fringes of *Landor's Tower*. Coney Beach, a fun-fair based on Coney Island - it was where a lot of miners went for holidays. Old villages stuck round and about and this school was on the edge of the sand dunes. It was completely out of Evelyn Waugh, that sort of period, just after the war - damaged schoolteachers with lumps of shrapnel in their head, spoiled priests... I enjoyed it actually [laughs]. It was a real culture shock to be dropped off there aged seven, not really knowing what was happening. But in a way, although it was harsh, it was a preparation for life, so that from then on I felt that I was OK wherever I was - If I'd survived this, I could survive anything.

Then, at nine, I was sent to Cheltenham, the prep school of the College, so that having been there I would presumably be qualified to go to the College when I was thirteen. Which I did. But that thing at nine was the biggest culture shock of all. Going away at seven was a surprise, but I was still within familiar territory and everybody in the school was Welsh, and it really wasn't that different from being at home. But when I went into the English middle class at nine, this was quite a thing, because I had a strong Welsh accent at the time, and they couldn't understand what I said. So suddenly everything was redefined - in the first school, I was top of the form and quite bright, but then everything turned right round when I arrived England. The work they did was of a very different kind, and the Latin was much more advanced and so on. As an outsider, you had to fight for survival, but once that period of adjustment was done, you were locked into this... minor prison for the next ten years.

KJ: Most of those friends of mine who went away to Public Schools, even to very liberal and enlightened schools, tend to say that on the whole they'd much rather have been day boys.

IS: I don't feel that really, because it would have been claustrophobic to have stayed in the society I was in. It was swings and roundabouts. A fairly ferocious experience, but on the other hand it gave me a sturdy independence, and I saw through a lot of the liberal pretensions of that time. At the prep school, they would have paintings by John Piper on the wall but they would beat you savagely; they would pontificate about apartheid while practising it enthusiastically on their own subjects. So I think at that time my sense of bullshit in English society comes in quite firmly...

KJ: That's quite an unusual experience, because at a lot of schools there's a much closer match between the public rhetoric and the grim reality of life...

IS: Not at all. That's what really got me. My first school was relatively benign - a fierce, rough and ready place - if you stepped out of line, bang! But there was no pretension. But in this English context, there was this grisly Bloomsbury overlay which only disguised a level of savagery that was worse than the Welsh one. I thought, "I don't believe a word of this." And I remember being naively straightforward and honest in lots of ways, they would say something, I'd reply and would get done for it, and I realised that to survive you have to get a bit more canny, street-wise, and disguise your motives. So I think my attitude to certain kinds of bullshit developed very young.

The School had a tradition - it's the school Lindsay Anderson went to, and Gavin Lambert, and Patrick White (I'm unusual in not being gay, I suppose) - a tradition of being very much a colonial, a military school. The naturalist who died on Scott's second expedition to the Antarctic, Dr Wilson, had been there, and he had a tiny museum in the school, full of threadbare penguins and pale watercolours of icebergs. So somewhere in the background was the ethos of preparing people to go out to distant lands, and the military ethic, bone- headed, hard-footed, was very much an aspect of the school. And yet there had been a slight liberal overlay - the Cheltenham Literary festival, music, all of that stuff was an element.

KJ: So this was something of an Orwell-at-Eton experience - becoming the precocious sceptic, becoming prematurely alive to hypocrisy.

IS: Yes, by the time I was thirteen I was wide awake... much, much cannier. Not unhappy, but I knew how it worked, and I was already a very strong believer in the view that if you want to do a thing, you do it yourself, you don't attempt to persuade them that this thing you're writing must go in their magazine, you form your own magazine. I don't wan't to do their plays, I'll do my own, make my own films... that was my attitude, and I operated as an independent society within this greater whole.

KJ: Presumably one thing that helped you thrive was that you were a decent athlete?

IS: Well, I was quite a ferocious fighter at my first school. I was more civilised by the time I was thirteen, because my natural aggression was channelled into rugby, hockey, cricket teams. Even so, I don't think that it really mattered - the sports thing wasn't an absolute element in the school. A lot of the people I knew there and got on well with were not at all sporting, I had a quite arbitrary range of friends. It wasn't, in that sense, a school which was all that much like Orwell's vision of Eton ... it wasn't a snobbish school, it was middle-of-the-road, unflashy, tweed jacket and sensible brown shoes. And there were different attitudes in the different Houses. I was in the most cowboy, quite a lot of Welsh people ... a remote outpost that went its own way. James Whittaker, the gossip columnist, was there just ahead of me and I think he was expelled. There was a slightly raffish, slightly off-centre bunch of people who came through.

KJ: So there was quite an agreeable side to the school?

IS: Yeah. I mean, I didn't like it much, I wouldn't choose it as a way of life, but it was tolerable.

KJ: You've said that some sense of vocation as a writer came at about the age of fourteen. What form did that take?

IS: Right from the start I was doing things, writing things, and then in the later years I would be publishing things. At some point, when I was about fifteen - again, this is that liberal thing - there was kind of a post Auden arty magazine that some of the brown tie and orange shirt masters had opened up, and I had a look at that and... well, I was already doing things that were more extreme, and they couldn't take them. So, funnily enough, I jumped into the mainstream school magazine and started putting poems about Ginsberg into it. Because they really didn't care, they were just filling the space, I was writing Dylan Thomas-y, apocalyptic things full of skulls and seas, and writing film reviews of Cocteau or whatever.

One thing which they did have which was worthwhile was a very good film society, so quite early on we got a mixture of films like Hitchcock's *Rear Window*, alongside Cocteau's *Orphée*, and we were allowed to go out and see films in the town - things like *Hiroshima, Mon Amour*, or Truffaut's *400 Blows* - and I also started getting away from school, hitching up to London and having binges of film viewing at the Academy Cinema. I began to see a lot. Also theatre, because it was quite a good time for English theatre. I wouldn't go near it now, but then there were Beckett and Brecht and Osborne and Pinter...

KJ: Did you ever experience a moment in adolescence like the one my friend Martin Wallen recalls, a precise moment when, as he puts it, unreflective childhood ways of thought ended and "consciousness dawned..."?

IS: Hmm. I guess there was, really. I can remember a visionary moment, or whatever you'd call it, of being awake at night. We slept in cubicles, wooden slatted cubicles... a limited amount of privacy, a bit box-like. I remember being in a hypnogogic state and having a vivid sense of being entombed in earth, and a series of voices or words came and announced themselves. And I scribbled them down, and that process of allowing these voices to come through was then part of my life from that moment onwards. I was about fourteen, fifteen.

KJ: Did you have any model of what it was to be a writer - say, a literary hero of some kind?

IS: Not really... Well, in a local sense, Dylan Thomas, because shortly after that experience I wrote a ...I couldn't call it a thesis, that would be too grand, but I had to write a piece about somebody, and I started to read a lot about Dylan Thomas, and also started to travel around Wales and meet people who had known him. I went to see Vernon Watkins, who was wonderful. He had actually grown up in Maesteg, where his father was the bank manager... I went out to see him in Pennard, where he lived, on the Gower, and he'd been a bit ill. He was in bed, wrapped up in a blazer, and he was very sympathetic. He'd been in a public school, Repton I think, and then he'd been in Cambridge...

KJ: Very briefly.

IS: Yes, he'd had a breakdown and left, became a character in Isherwood's book [*Lions and Shadows*], so he had a very good sense of what I was. He gave me a terrific evening talking about his vocation as a poet, and also being a bank clerk, the two lives which didn't impinge, and the whole back story of Dylan Thomas as well, and then looking at these photographs of Dylan Thomas playing croquet in the garden in Pennard as a very young man. And then I went to Laugharne- where Thomas is buried - and went to the pub and talked to people who knew him, got the whole story, took millions of photographs - very much the way I work now. So I wrote this piece, stuck photographs all over it, and that focused something which was very much in my consciousness. His background is close to my mother's family background, exactly the same places: Swansea Uplands, Mumbles, Worm's Head, Ferryside, New Quay, the same people. They all knew each other in Swansea. His father taught in the grammar school in Swansea. So Dylan Thomas was the model, in a sense - not knowing exactly how the story went, but knowing that he'd got away to London, and that was what you had to do.

KJ: Did the examples of Vernon Watkins and Thomas make you think more exactly about what you might find to do as a day job to support your writing?

IS: I never really thought about that, quite honestly. I assumed I'd do something, but I never bothered to think what it was, until a notion evolved that I might be able to make some kind of living out of cinema, which was the other thing I wanted to do. My twin passions, really, were poetry and cinema. Dylan Thomas was the initial model, but I soon moved on to Eliot, Pound, Hitchcock, Buñuel, Orson Welles.

KJ: How easy was it at that time to come by texts by, say, Ginsberg, if you weren't living in a metropolitan centre and moving in vaguely avant-garde circles?

IS: Fairly easy. I had one good English teacher, as one traditionally is supposed to do, but it didn't come at that point where it could have changed my life, because I was already there and I didn't agree with him about lots of things. He was called Jim Greenwood, and he'd been a famous rugby player for Scotland and the British Lions, playing in their victory against The Springboks. So he came to the school with that background, which is why they took him on, but in fact he was very, very good on English literature, passionate about it, it was the real passion of his life. One of his beliefs was that you should read everything, you should always have a pile of books on the go, and he threw dozens of things at me, some of which went nowhere, but he gave me a paperback of Kerouac, *Maggie Cassidy*, the first edition, the paperback original published by Panther in

1960, and I devoured it. And then there was an anthology called *The Beat Generation and the Angry Young Men,* which had just come out in paperback. The Burroughs thing was pseudonymous, attributed to 'William Lee', but I picked up on that, and my parents had just gone on holiday for the first time to America, gone to New York, and they asked me what I wanted brought back. So I gave them a reading list - they had to go down to the Village and find *The Dharma Bums...* [laughs] So, there you are, I read all that stuff when I was about seventeen.

KJ: It was the Beats who were most important to you?

IS: Yes, the Angry Young Man part of the book never convinced me in the slightest - John Wain and all that...I just thought, "Jesus, what is this?" [Laughs.] But the other stuff, the Beats - just the nature of the prose, the language, the sense of recording everything. Very Romantic, obviously.. And then shading into Burroughs' dystopian satires, all of which was very appealing. So I did my own home-work, read everything, and by the time I left Cheltenham I was quite well read in that area, and also widely, but thinly, informed as to cinema and theatre.

KJ: How about music?

IS: Music, no. I mean, I listened to the things that came through, but it wasn't a passion. Funnily enough, a friend of mine was a guy called Andy Wickham, a very skilled cartoonist who went on to be the first publicist for the Rolling Stones. He was passionate about music - blues, rock and roll, all that stuff, and I got it from him. I was interested... I mean, I was also interested in Zen Buddhism, reading Dr Suzuki, so we were exchanging snippets of misinforma-tion. This was a time when Brian Jones was around in Cheltenham, and we knew about him, there was a good interaction with the town, we weren't locked in, and I was aware of that Rolling Stones stuff coming up, but it wasn't a passion of my life. I was also following on hints in Kerouac, listening to Bebop - I liked that.

KJ: I suppose that generally I don't associate you very much with an interest in music, at least not the mainstream variety. About the only connection that comes to mind would be the sort of fringe, experimental rock musicians who take part in performances like your Barbican M25 event - Scanner, The KLF people...

IS: Well, they've always come to me, and obliquely, via a guy called Paul Smith, a concert promoter and secret genius behind the 'Blast First' and 'King Mob' labels. I wouldn't have come across them otherwise. I really like listening to it - Bruce Gilbert of Wire, particularly, I find amazing, I find his hungry way with sound obsessive and mind-warping. He's been vital to the films we've done with Chris Petit...

KJ: There's something of a prejudice among people who weren't adult or even alive then that the fifties were an apallingly dreary time - grey, boring, culturally undernourished... not a good time to be young.

IS: Actually it was quite exciting culturally, because we were getting rumours of the American underground coming in, untainted by the political agenda that even by the mid-sixties I was getting very dubious about. What we were really reading about were things that had happened in the late forties, and while I was still in school I got caught up in Jackson Pollock and action painting. I started to paint drip canvases, did lots of them and got very obsessive, and I'd hang them up on my walls. This man Jim Greenwood came and saw them, said "My God", and put on an exhibition of these Pollockian pictures, which were the absolute anthithesis of... I mean, I would never have had a painting accepted into the official school art days, which were always nice watercolours, landscapes and genteel abstractions... So I was very interested in American Abstract Expressionism, and realised that you could do it, you didn't have to buy the line that was being promoted - this Piper stuff, Graham Sutherland. We were given all that but we weren't offered, say,

29

Francis Bacon. So when I went to London shortly after this time and the big Bacon exhibition was at the Tate, it blew me away completely, I thought, well, why haven't I heard about this man? This is amazing!

KJ: Have you preserved any of your writings from school?

IS: [Laughs] Well, I can't remember chucking them out. I've got this lock-up in Whitechapel which is just packed... a compacted block, and all that stuff is in there somewhere, whatever survives of it I don't know. Cans of film, too...

KJ: Will you be flogging it to Austin, Texas?

IS: I'd love to. That's the dream, that one day some one will come, take the whole lot away, and hand over money.

★★★

PART TWO:

FILM SCHOOL, DUBLIN,
EARLY DAYS IN LONDON

KJ: So, you would have been about eighteen when you first moved to London?

IS: Yes, I came to the London School of Film Technique in Brixton. It wasn't even a full-year course, it was just under a year. I'd just left school, I wasn't even that keen to go to university, though I knew there was an underlying expectation to do this, but I was much more keen to get to London and move into the film world in some way. I thought, well, if you go to film school, you can get the bones of the matter technically and then see where you go from there. Because it was an exciting period - not in England, particularly...

KJ: This was about 1961? The first *nouvelle vague* films coming through?

IS: I'd seen them, thought, well, this could happen in England. Because there's [Lindsay] Anderson, Karl Reisz and whoever running about, and there's a crossover betwen theatre and Free Cinema... there's a sense that the doors might open. [The play-wright] Arnold Wesker has been in this film school just before me, his magazines are still sitting around there, and the school's titular head - I hardly ever see him - is a man called Robert Dunbar - who takes you into Ed Dorn and Marianne Faithfull and all of that family. [Robert Dunbar's son John, married at the time to Marianne Faithfull, ran the Indica Gallery, mainly remembered today as the place where John Lennon first met Yoko Ono. The American poet Ed Dorn later married John Dunbar's sister.] Anyway, I can remember landing up in Brixton, in Electric Avenue, where the school was above a butcher's shop. I came down there on a Sunday and was walking around wearing a black shirt, and this copper put a hand on my shoulder and said "You can't wear that round here, son". It had never impinged on me that this race thing was still active and a real concern. Brixton was pretty black, then, and there was a lot of fascist material round the edge of it.

KJ: I'd always associated Mosley's blackshirts with East London, not South...

IS: No.. When I was there, looking around newsagents' windows for a place to stay, there were cards saying "No Blacks, No Irish" everywhere... Landladies were terribly pleased to get a white, middle-class, nicely spoken person, threw their places open. There was a lot of edge, but on the other hand the general culture was really great, free and easy.. No real tension of any sort that I noticed, it was a great place to live. But this copper said, "You can't live here, son, not in Brixton. Take the bus to the next stop out." So I ended up in West Norwood, which was a wonderfully dozy suburb. But it was a nice sense of South London, all those evangelical churches and quiet avenues. You'd get the bus into Brixton, spend the day there...

KJ: Was it exciting to be out of school at last?

IS: Oh, yes. I just literally walked out of the door and wiped it. Bang. That was it. No sense of terrible ghosts to exorcise, it didn't bite that deeply into me. That's it, thank you, done that, let's get on, this is the real business.

KJ: Does a school of that kind teach you to live very much inside your own head?

IS: I think it does. I think the thing of having lived in a foreign country, in an alien environment for so long... so much of the material of your real personality is suppressed. The people I was playing rugby with were very suspicious of me publishing poetry,

34

and equally the poetry people didn't like me playing rugby, so there was a sort of schizophrenia about it, you were not quite yourself in either world. Although actually a lot of the hearties were freaky and interesting individuals anyway... But I think it gave you that sense of being able to go through on auto-pilot, do what you had to do, but you were never engaging the real gears. So being in London there was a feeling of shedding that, and trying to come to some real self that fitted into an environment.

KJ: Did you have a grant to attend film school?

IS: No. It didn't cost very much, and I persuaded my parents to pay for it. I lived really, really cheaply - rent was some pitifully small amount...

KJ: Your rather barbed account of your time at the school in "Cinema Purgatorio" suggests that you didn't learn very much there.

IS: No, technically it was a disaster. The whole thing was on the point of collapse. There were all kinds of things going on, the equipment was being smuggled out and used in porn movies or whatever and would end up with crooks. The only teaching was second rate... there was an old, quite well-known film director called Maurice Elvey, who had made H.G. Wells-type stuff and had been a noted figure in his day, but was now absolutely like an ancient actor-manager. He came in with a hat and coat, and would say, "Oh, in cinema you can do anything, you can open a door here and you can step out into the alps...." An hour at a time of vague reminiscences, but it was just not what I needed or wanted. On the other hand, we did get to make the odd film, because there was a camera, there was film stock... you taught yourself. I got to write and direct one film on 16mm...

KJ: What was it like?

IS [Laughs]: It was a fairly grisly, right-on fable about a middle-class black guy. Think of *Shadows* or Losey's *The Damned*. I was the only English student there, most of the students were Nigerians or Malayans or Egyptians who would reckon to go back and take their place in the government. They were very suited and clean and businesslike - they'd have had laptops now. So I interposed one of these guys into the Brixton culture, in his three-piece tweed suit. He gets stabbed by a gang, hoodlums in leather jackets... The thing was to shoot in the streets, in the Market.

That was more or less finished, and then we took off to Spain and went to Pamplona and made a documentary about the bull run. Lived down there for a few weeks, usually drunk - all this Hemigway stuff. The film was no good, really, but it was an account of that festival.

KJ: Did you ever seriously think that you had a chance for a big movie career?

IS: No. The only career that would have been feasible then, with that, was moving into the BBC as Third Assistant Editors. Programmes were still being made on film, and you'd spend your time winding reels backwards and forwards, being the equivalent of a chemist's assistant. Coming from that kind of background, you entree would have to have been on the technical level. It's not as if you'd come out of Oxford or Cambridge with a Footlights reputation, and could go into writing and directing. What you would have been expected to do was assistant camera, clapper-board or editing. The way I would have gone was editing, and this wasn't what I wanted at all. So I was quite prepared to duck the issue by going to university.

KJ: So the Film School was really a kind of Gap Year?

IS: I didn't think of it that way, but that was what it became. Living on your own in the city, being part of this group at Film School...

KJ: And then to Trinity College, Dublin - a time you've hardly written about at all, except very briefly. Why Dublin?

IS: Obvious reasons. Largely because it was very easy to get into. Secondly because I fancied the idea of living in Dublin, on the back of [J.P. Donleavy's novel] *The Ginger Man*. And on a more serious level, the Beckett, Joyce, Flann O'Brien mythology. I thought, this is the place to be - a place where you could just live, hide out, without the university impinging too much upon you. And that was perfectly true. The university didn't impinge on me at all. It was four years of experimentation, a four-year exercise in trying out theatre, film, writing of all sorts, and interesting social inter-actions. The academic part of it hardly took up ten minutes of my time.

KJ: Officially you were reading English?

IS: English and Fine Arts. I quite enjoyed the European Art History courses.

KJ: So did you live a *Ginger Man* style of existence?

IS: In a sense. There were a lot of periods which were pretty drunken because the whole culture was, basically, the bar. If you wanted to go into such and such a bar off Grafton Street, there was Patrick Kavanagh at this end, and there was Flann O'Brien.. You could see them. Behan was around, he was already dying, visibly, in these bars, being drunk to death by American well-wishers who would send drinks over. All the poets were visible and could be known and seen and heard.

KJ: Did you hang out with a particular crowd, a gang, as it were?

IS: Well, as it were. It was very much like now: the official poetry culture of the place was Derek Mahon and Michael Longley and Eavan Boland and Brendan Kennelly - I knew them, loosely, on a nodding basis, and published with them in this magazine, although

I was obviously the enemy of that type of writing - this rhetorical, Irish gestural stuff, very heavy Yeatsian/Louis MacNeice tonalities, and I was pitching Charles Olson and William Carlos Williams and Pound and Zukovsky... I hadn't read Olson until I got to Dublin, I realised there was a trajectory between the Beats and Black Mountain, and I started to read Black Mountain stuff in Dublin. There were big piles of *Poetry Chicago*, and Dublin bookshops were very good at getting American imports. I can remember buying Olson's *The Distances* in a bookshop on O'Connell Street - unimaginable now, but there was all this Compendium-type material just turning up in an ordinary bookshop.

KJ: I have the impression that Olson made a big impact on you.

IS: Very big impact. I would say that he became the major figure for me and a number of people, so that when we began publishing magazines, this was a kind of looming presence... we published sections from the *Maximus* poems. It was the sense of somebody... a very, very large presence, obviously, a drama of his own persona, a sense of somebody nailing down a sea town and opening it up to the world. And being pretentious students, the list of reading matter was very exciting, I loved all that...

KJ: Carl Sauer..

IS:...all of that was very appealing. Olson and Robert Duncan, Creeley and Dorn and various acolytes and followers of that school were the people that meant most.

KJ: What was your own poetry like at this period?

IS: I wrote a huge amount in the period when I was in London, a vast Eliotic epic. I can't remember exactly what it was like, but I know that there was a lot of collage material... it had a section that cross-cut late Yeats "Byzantium" with Mickey Spillane. [Laughs] Because I was also interested in pulp *noir* fiction which you could pick up in Popular Book Centres. Already, I very much liked mixing junky American pulp with the most Golden Dawn-ish poetic things, bringing the two together. So I'd written huge epics of this type, and I'd even thought about doing a book, because I had a lot of pages piling up, and I assembled it and thought, ... no, this is absurd at this point. But I had volumes and volumes of poetry written.

KJ: So the Dylan Thomas was out of your system, and you'd become a kind of Black Mountaineer...

IS: Something on the cusp; my own strange version, quite surreal and savage. The Dylan Thomas rhetoric was gone, but I hadn't the discipline of the Olsonian, Black Mountain, scholarly thing, it was a much weirder form... very film-influenced, very visual. So I got started on this Dublin magazine called *Icarus*, a terrible thing, but luckily for me there was one editor who was not part of that Mahon/Longley set-up, and he very much took to what I did, so I got fast-streamed into this thing by something I sent him. He said, "Oh, this is amazing, we've got to do a reading..." I thought, give a poetry reading? I hardly knew what a poetry reading was! So here I was, reading this strange stuff out virtually the first minute I arrived in the place. Because of that, I got put on the committee of this magazine, which meant that you only had to survive to become the editor, so I just bided my time, let all this other stuff pass. You were only allowed to do one term as editor, so just by sitting back and waiting I finally got the thing into my hands.

KJ: And so the Sinclair Mad Issue came out...

IS: It was a crazy issue. The cover was a comic strip that Tim Booth, who was one of [the sixties folk rock group] Dr. Strangely Strange, drew, in which the Icarus figure was cast as Batman - zap! All that pop art thing. And it had a big chunk of Burroughs in the middle of it, which could be read in three columns, down or across... the effect of all this in Dublin was incredible! The next issue - because I had infiltrated a tranche of other, like-minded people - this next issue was banned outright, not allowed to be sold. It's quite collectable now, because it was one of the first magazines to publish Seamus Heaney. Not me, but one of the other people had come across him somewhere, and because it was banned, it must be a very collectable Heaney item.

KJ: What were the proportions of working to boozing and messing around?

IS: Well, like now, I worked quite hard. Made about four films, wrote two plays - one of them in a night. There was a very nice little theatre that the University had, and we looked at the productions that other people were doing, and they were the kind of people who would spend the rest of their lives appearing in B-features or on televsion. With this other character, a friend of mine, called Chris Bamford, we wrote the first play in a matter of about three days, by a process of going to separate rooms and writing stuff and then banging it together, and then cutting in reams of found material from all over. We staged it by lighting it with huge electric torches, and having posters and photos and bits of film and dancers.. The whole thing was like a mad happening. It was called... [long pause] I've forgotten. [Another long pause.] *An Explanation*, it was called *An Explanation*, and it went into the Dublin Theatre Festival in a double bill with an Irish *Under Milk Wood* [Laughs.] That was hilarious. The establishment of the place thought it was pretentious and monstrous and appalling in every way, but I remember going into a Chinese restaurant and [the theatre director] Max Stafford-Clark was there, and he came across and said "Wonderful, marvellous, dear boy..." He was a student concurrently with us, he'd directed [Max Frisch's] *The Fire Raisers*, but he was the only one who had the nous to recognise that this strange fringe happening had a kind of demented poetic that was of some interest.

```
                    5th Annual U.D.A. Festival 1963
                          hosts:  U.C.D.

                        CHANGE OF PROGRAMME

  Wed. 13th    Glasgow University will not present  "Waiting for Godot"

                        _____

  Non Competitive Entries:-

           Trinity College, Dublin  present  AN EXPLANATION
           with a dramatic prologue and epilogue.
                    Written and produced by
              Christopher Bamford and Ian Sinclair.
                          with

           Anna Hadman              Heather Lukes
           Sue McHarg               Penny Oakley
           Ivan Pawle               Hilary Fildes
           Peter Bowles             David Durrell
           Nickolas Crickman        Martin Benham
           Henry Prosser            Christopher Bamford
                    and Ian Sinclair

              Lighting:  Tom Baker.

           University College, Dublin, present  "Under Milk Wood"
           a play for voices by  Dylan Thomas.

           Voices: (from left to right)
           Sunniva O'Neill, Colm O'Briain, Margaret Hughes,
           Macdara Woods, David Jordon, Margaret Harrington
           Eamonn Grennan.
```

After this event had gone on, I was in a late-night pub and met this actor, one of the very fruitiest of the establishment actors, who said "OOOOh, hmm, provocative language in there but it needs proper actors, direction. You write something serious and I'll do it." So with Chris Bamford, we set off from this pub, somewhat pissed, and went on this huge walk through the night, through Dublin, arguing it out, and arrived back at Sandymount where we lived in a house on the sea, got two typewriters, started work at about three, four in the morning and, using layers of duplicating paper, so many that the bottom copy was almost illegible, whacked this play out. By nine o'clock in the morning it was finished, and when this actor woke up in his rooms, the draft of the play was already there. We gave copies to Ralph Bates, who went on to star in Hammer horror films, and Constantine de Goguel, Chris Serle and all the other exotic names we could locate... all these local acting stars, all of them when they woke up in the morning had this invisible script waiting on their doorstep.

KJ: What was this second play about?

IS: This was a much more Beckettian thing, I suppose it was in the vein of *Endgame*, slightly - *very* pretentious, *Lear*, *Endgame*, very operatic, with enormous ranting arias that went on for pages and much more quick-fire knockabout as well. We staged this one ourselves - we got a little theatre, because Ireland was full of little garage theatres, and put this play on for the public with one of our films.

I've got a cutting, the listings page from from the evening paper in Dublin: at The Gate Theatre, Bernard Shaw at The Garrick, *A Taste of Honey*, Samuel Beckett, blah blah blah, and then at the bottom of the page is this thing! It went on, and the Dublin critics came and reviewed it, and Ivan Pawle, who was one of Dr Strangely Strange, acted in it, and a woman called Dinah Stabb, who I think is a very good actress, and went on to act with Gielgud, but this was her first part. It ran for about a week - we got a proper director in to direct it, and he was drowning, basically, [laughs], because it needed Fritz Lang direction, dictatorial, megalomaniac, inspired.

It was called *Cords*. An image of a central, Lear figure with intestinal cords going to lots of lesser creatures who infuriate him and interact with him.

Commencing on Nov. 23rd for 6 nights at 8-15 p.m.

You are invited to

CORDS AND DISCHORDS

by

C.G.E.BAMFORD & I.M.SINCLAIR

Director: I.H.MILTON

EYE THEATRE CLUB

Strand Road, Sandymount

No. 3 Bus, beside Convent   Tickets 4s 6d

KJ: Can you remember much about the four films you made in the Dublin period? Their names, for instance, if they had names?

IS: Oh yes, they had names. One was a sort of [Roman Polanksi's] *Two Men and a Wardrobe*-type film called *After*, which was all shot in derelict industrial landscapes in Wales, very post-apocalyptic, like Alex Garland and Danny Boyle with zero budget. It had one nice shot in it - a graveyard, a cross-tracking shot to a figure on top of a grave who whips off his dark glasses to reveal other glasses beneath... but most of it is just high-flown rubbish. It was dedicated to Anthony Mann (and *The Naked Spur*). Then there was some kind of vaguely... Losey (post-*Servant*) thing shot in London, whose name I've forgotten... yes, called 'Stasis'... which was the one where I found myself ringing up Mandy Rice-Davies, because it was in that era [of the Profumo scandal]... it was a strange, louche, London thing. Botched orgies in South Kensington bed-sits. Then there was one I made with Tom Baker, either called *Them* or *They*, I can't remember, which was not bad, because it was just straight documentation, watching the streets of Dublin, filming from the car - the night streets of Dublin. It had harmonica music by Larry Adler's son, who did the music for that Losey film. [*King and Country*].. And then there was another one, partly Dublin, partly London, it had *Lazarus* in the title somewhere, *Breakfast of Lazarus* maybe - much more French, Godardian, lots of Brechtian devices like someone coming towards you with a big sheet of glass you don't see and he writes "DETACH" on it. All kinds of script and text in it, and it cross-cuts a lot from black and white to colour...It was more or less cut together, but never really saw the light of day.

KJ: Were these all made in university vacations or in term time?

IS: Oh, there was no distinction between the two.

KJ: Since you've mentioned Godard, and thinking of his increasingly politicisation during the 1960s, were you a political animal in those days?

IS: No, no... politics came after this period, when we'd left Dublin to come back to London - more or less at the time of the *Kodak Mantra Diaries*, when I was making the film with Ginsberg in 1967, and there was that whole business of the Congress of the Dialectics of Liberation.. Hearing all this rhetoric day after day, meeting people living in squats, getting a different story,... and the Situationists, I remember those Situationist booklets popping up at that time.

As an undergraduate I was pretty apolitical. Mostly still going deeply into the Black Mountain poets, old Hollywood and current European cinema, that sort of world, rather than political reality, because in a sense it was a spoiled existence - not having to work, living modestly, a sort of bohemian, threadbare existence with no pressures of any kind, and just experimenting with various things.

KJ: These were still pre-hippie days, though?

IS: At the very end of this period, dope began to creep across the horizon... A lot of people were into cough medicine, that sort of thing, but only in the last year or so.

KJ: So was it more in the nature of a timeless Dublin bohemia to which you were the latest recruits?

IS: Yes, I think there was that, very much so. I don't think there'd been any real shift in this period from the society that Donleavy was depicting in *The Ginger Man* - it's the same sort of thing, run-down boarding houses, bars in the cattle market that were open all day, an endless dialogue running around these pubs, and people going out of town to some pub open on a hill - that was the life...

KJ: You found it congenial?

IS: Well... relatively congenial.

KJ: What was the limitation?

IS: I never wanted to piss my life away in a pub. I just didn't. I really have a puritanical thing: in the morning, you get up, you write, you do your stuff, you get on. This other thing was... interesting, but it was never going to be deeply attractive to me.

KJ: How about academic work? Did you read a lot?

IS: Well, I read a lot of comics...[laughs]

KJ: How about, oh, I don't know, say....Heidegger?

IS: I wasn't reading Heidegger... but no, I did read quite a lot. Substantial quantities of quite abstruse poetry - American, English, European.

KJ: Who exactly? Paul Celan?

IS: Celan, certainly. Rimbaud, in French with a crib... and lots of those people that Olson suggests. I was reading about paleontology, stone circles, economic currents - reading widely and crazily. Not a lot of novels, other than the things you were supposed to read for the course..

KJ: So, you studied the likes of Frobenius...

IS: Absolutely, Frobenius... And D.H. Lawrence, Burroughs...

KJ: Were you thinking of writing novels?

IS: I wrote quite a lot of short prose pieces, and I'd written a sort of novel when I was still in film school - I'd plotted it through, quite carefully, and it's just as well plotted or un-plotted as anything I do now. I'd worked it out in great detail, and I wrote five or six chapters, and then realised that I didn't have the technical where-withal to deliver what I wanted to do. I saw how it worked, I saw the way that it was set up - it was, again, based on the sense of London I was getting in Brixton, and then moves off into a more Express-ionist landscape. Drives lifted from *Lolita*. If I could have written it, it would have been a reasonably workmanlike novel. So, yes, there was a sense of wanting to write a novel, too, but I never did. I began that one, abandoned it, and didn't do another one until quite some time later.

KJ: Were you a very noticeable figure as an undergraduate? A local legend?

IS: Oh no, no, far from. There was a large group of people, but no notable guru figure within the group. I think I was one of the most active in terms of doing things, but there were more notable figures in the pub or whatever who were seen as the artists of the time. In terms of delivering, I was one of the busiest... There really wasn't any sense of career in this group. There was, I'm sure, for, say Derek Mahon and Michael Longley, who were already having quite substantial poetic careers, they were known in America, getting the poetry prizes, and would have been in the system already, at that time...I think really, my group was just interested in living the life, very easy-going. If I was doing something I could drag them in, but they'd just as soon sit around somewhere drinking. It was a culture based on talk and quiet movement, loads and loads of talk and sitting around drinking and parties - there wasn't a lot of producing, and certainly no sense of "We should make these moves to create a future career." A lot of this group would have ended up just drifting to the West of Ireland and staying there, never moving on...

The choice really was, for this lot, either going to the west of Ireland and living the life - because they were more intersted in spiritual dimensions and pre-hippie dope culture - or you would move to America. And that was more appealing to me. I could easily have gone to America at that time, I was right on the edge of that.

KJ: What happened immediately after graduation?

IS: I just carried on, there was no real break. I got my degree. I went to London, finished up making this fourth film I've mentioned in black and white and colour, and then started to find a job and somewhere to live. I tried various things, and the first one which came up was teaching in this North East London Polytechnic place, in Walthamstow. I started out teaching everything to Day Release students - you know, General Studies, how to write a letter. And then during the course of the year, a guy teaching film studies there, an old American leftist who'd been black-listed and come over, and was always depressed as hell... he got seriously ill, and gave up, so I took over his job and started teaching film, which was very interesting and leads on to all sorts of other things.

KJ: Well, for one thing, you mention in *Lights Out* that this was the time and place when you first met your long-term friend and partner in crime Brian Catling...

IS: It was an inspired generation of drop-outs from all the sink schools of London, who ended up going there, most of whom had something going for them. Brian Catling was the most notable of all the arts students I met when I took over the film course; even at that point, he knew very precisely the kinds of film he wanted to make. He'd made this film before I met him, a sort of Warholesque film, I guess you'd call it, which was someone projectile vomiting for an entire reel. Then, as now, he loved a static camera, a steady stare. The victim been given a spaghetti dinner and then dosed with salt water... and then the other kinds of films Catling was doing were obsessively to do with Battle of Britain pilots and psychosis, all set in South London, dingy inner city housing set-ups, colours of wallpaper, colours of pyjamas...He had his own universe that he followed. He'd known [the sculptor] Steve Dilworth at Maidstone before this, and lived off road-kill in a strange house with a dwarf and a nymphomaniac... it sounds like a sixties play by Ann Jellicoe [*laughter*] but it was really the case.

And as I got to know Catling, he started to call round to the house in Hackney on Fridays, because he was living on nothing, and he'd worked out a routine where he could get fed here on Friday night, move on to his girlfriend's on Saturday night and get fed there, get home for Sunday dinner in Camberwell and survive for another week. And then, soon after that, we both worked in Truman's brewery...

KJ: From the oblique references you make to this Walthamstow time in your books, it sounds like an unexpectedly fertile period. How long did the job last? A year?

IS: It all becomes very grey, because after this there's a ten-year period running from the mid-sixties to the mid-seventies, during which nothing is fixed, no proper harbours. In the early days I was teaching part-time, and also writing and film-making, just making enough to live on. I was married then, quite young...

KJ: You met Anna, your wife, in Dublin?

49

IS: In Dublin. She was in the first play... we got married at 23. For that generation it was not unusually young, a lot of students were married. So we were living in one room in Hampstead and she was going off to work at Unilever, I was going off to teach at Walthamstow and otherwise beginning the process of wandering around London and writing, which started then. Freud's ashes in Golders Green to Karl Marx's effigy in Highgate, and St Pancras Old Church, and out along the canal to Hackney, Victoria Park. At the end of that initial period, the film with Ginsberg came through. I'd had this friend at film school, a Dutchman called Robert Klinkert, who asked me for ideas, what could we do? I mentioned the Congress of the Dialectics of Liberation coming up, and he said that it sounded very interesting, so I wrote a half-page, it went off with a load of other ideas, and West German TV said, yes, we'll pay for that.

★★★

PART THREE:

DIALECTICS OF LIBERATION TO
ALBION VILLAGE PRESS

KJ: You once suggested that meeting Ginsberg was a huge event, something that really turned things around for you...

IS: It didn't so much turn things around... As I explained earlier, one evening spent talking with Vernon Watkins... there was a sense of genealogy in this business of Anglo-Welsh poets, that I'd connect up in part with painters like Ceri Richards, as well. A sense of Gower, a sense of place, of archetypal meanings hovering over a landscape. I thought, here's a tradition that I can connect with, and is going to come back in my life at some point. Meeting Ginsberg, the extraordinary thing was that though he'd never been a hero of mine in the sense that Kerouac and Burroughs had been - I thought he was more of an operator, interesting, but... - still, here was one of those figures from this early imaginative landscape actually in the flesh, live, and the jump of seeing someone you'd read all these accounts of in Kerouac's novels, you'd read interviews, read *Howl*, and *Kaddish*, and now here he is!

And the sense of that public role, and political engagement of the poet, the availability of this man, prepared to meet strangers out of the blue who've just turned up on the doorstep and generously give his time...

KJ: My experience of Ginsberg, who I met several times between the late seventies and early nineties, was rather different, more disillusioning. I'm afraid the words that come to mind would be pompous, priggish, self-important...

IS: Yeah, I guess that was there, but that didn't appear to be the important element. He was being very Messianic....It was an exciting point in the culture, in that there were massive poetry readings, and suddenly there were all these poeple like John Berryman, Olson was on stage... all these people gathered from the four corners of the world. And then in this railway shed [the Roundhouse, Camden] there were all the newer figures I'd been getting into, like [R.D.] Laing, Stokeley Carmichael, Paul Goodman, David Cooper - they were all there, and Ginsberg bridged the two worlds, and he's also obsessively interested in the glamour of the rock and roll thing, he's after McCartney and Mick Jagger. He's got a red shirt that's been painted by Paul McCartney, and he's in Hyde Park, leading dope rallies ... it's bogus but it's real, it's crazy, and everything seems to be opening, splitting in new ways.

KJ: The most generous thing you said about Ginsberg was that talking to him for a few days gave you material to think about for the next few years.

IS: I think it did...the whole experience of those few weeks around the Congress was so intense - a lot of people arriving out of nowhere and sleeping on our floor - we were living in Belsize Park... and they were coming from across Europe, from Dublin...

people were living in the Roundhouse, there were arguments and debates, and you'd go out to the back and suddenly you were having to talk to R.D. Laing, interview him, and he takes you back to his house...

The heat of it was extraordinary: whoompf! Out of nowhere, out of something that had been very slow and dozy and gradual through the Dublin years...

KJ: A catalytic moment?

IS: A catalytic moment. I realised then that this explosive thing was going to carry through into the mid-seventies. And, again, at the same time as Ginsberg and the Dialectics of Liberation and all that, there was an extraordinary change in attitudes. People who in Dublin had been involved in music, with Dr Strangely Strange or The Incredible String Band, had now become part of Baader-Meinhof, or on the fringes of that.

And in London, we were soon involved, through a guy who at the time was a night porter at the Metropolitan Hospital in Kingsland Road - which is now gone, it's a series of workshops and offices - anyway, I got to know fringes of the Angry Brigade set-up. He was a strange, weird little troublemaker: he took us into the hospital at night, opened drawers and showed us corpses... The Angry Brigade people were all in Stoke Newington - not the main people, but other ones. And that led into a nexus of the squatting movement up in Redhill, and we went in and filmed a lot of the houses that were barricaded and were being charged by bailiffs. We got into these meetings, and were hearing conversations in obscure kitchens about people who were making bombs - that was the debate. Incidentally, one of the convicted Angry Brigade people, Anna Mendelson - whom I didn't meet at this time - re-invented herself when she came out of prison as Grace Lake, and I think is a very good poet, a considerable figure, who produces streams of substantial work.

And in Hackney, on the Balls Pond Road, were these people called the Exploding Galaxy Commune - they were being written up in *IT* - the *International Times* - and there was a sense of aliens of various kinds landing up in the deserts of Hackney/Stoke Newington and actually plotting political actions, political theatre, on a serious stage. We heard a lot of that, took part in debates, including some with some quite interesting anarchist groups. The only people who seemed to have any real ideas were Dutch. They were older, more mature and they'd done things with the Provos. I used to drive their main guy around, quite a lot, through Whitechapel, because they used the Anarchist Freedom Bookshop in Angel Alley. I remember, vividly, one night, taking him down there, and there was a whole warehouse building just full of people in sleeping bags, with candles burning, and a real sense that they're going to go out into the City and do extraordinary things. But the English never really responded - they preferred sitting around talking, discussing, and going to the pub and having meetings. This Dutch guy was all for direct action, but nobody followed it up.

I also went to the Vietnam demonstration in Grosvenor Square - again, more or less as an interested observer. It was very genteel, and then all of a sudden it turned savage, and I could see these massive police horses charging... I had another sense of the State, and how American politics were protected in a serious way... Whereas I'd gone along, in general sympathy, just for an interesting gathering of people.

Later, in the early Seventies, that sort of political element carried over into real politics. I was working in what was left of the docks - the docks were collapsing, and the work moved into these container sheds at Stratford East, which some cowboys were operating as a way of getting round the intransigence of the Trades Unions and restrictive practices in the docks. So without knowing we were involved in it, we got taken on as easy, cheap labour to work loading and unloading containers. And then this became a major political force when the dockers blockaded it, strikes were called, all kinds of stuff went on. So I then saw the other side, the real nitty-gritty politics of people who were involved through their lives and their work.

KJ: So did that help deepen your scepticism about the likes of the Angry Brigade?

IS: I was always sceptical - I mean, some of the people you met were so preposterous, so theatrical and ultimately paranoid - peeping out of windows, hiding behind curtains. But some of the real old-time Communists I met were very striking people. They were serious, they were really in it for the long-term. They were jokey about their paranoia, but it was true that when one of them visited the house, there was a car, following him around - they were Enemies of the State. So those people were quite impressive, but the bogus ones were just like really bad actors, and seemed to live in very prissy conditions, with His-and-Hers mugs on hooks, but talking about doing these ludicrous things...

KJ: It strikes me that you're not one of nature's joiners...

IS: No, that's true. Very true. [Laughs]

KJ: You never joined a political party?

IS: No.... The nightmare of my life is to be in a meeting where things are debated, for hours. Though the experience of being at the Roundhouse, at the Congress, was different, and very interesting. There were little groups all over the place holding these quite ferocious discussions. People like [Alex] Trocchi were there, with the Sigma Portfolio. Laing was being quite Messianic... you had a sense that things could change, things could be done. And then of course it petered out into general malcontent and lethargy in the seventies, but in the sixties there was a very brief period of activity, from which the more extreme people went into violent action. And we were debating violent action, but I just wasn't going to do that. It wasn't part of my remit. I thought it was wrong at the time - showbiz rather than anything else.

KJ: So did you regard yourself in that context primarily as a documentarian?

IS: Yes, I think that was really in my head all along. I thought this should be documented and remembered, but I'm not going to seriously get involved with it.

KJ: Was Gregory Bateson an impressive figure?

IS: I think that in many ways, and to most of the people there, he was one of the most impressive. He was the figure they were all talking about. He was doing this thing about the melting polar ice-caps - which hadn't been discussed at that time - and he was also very sensible and English, he wasn't doing an impassioned rock'n'roll performance, it was just straightforward delivery. And the material he brought up was the most gripping, I thought... because Stokeley Carmichael was kind of embarrassing, rhythm and blues, rock race rant, and Emmett Grogan [of the Diggers] was sunken into drug-induced state catatonia, with dark glasses... all of that was pretty grisly.

KJ: Did you find it so at the time, or is this partly a matter of retrospect?

IS: No, I did find it grisly at the time. There was a lot... there were acres of bullshit around. Some element of that is in the book, *Kodak Mantra Diaries*, I think - people spouting this rhetoric who quite clearly in a few years were going to be merchant bankers, you could see it clearly then.

KJ: To move on slightly from fringe political idelogies to other kinds of unconventional or counter-cultural beliefs - the whole spiritual, metaphysical side of the sixties, from geomancy to shaman-ism or what have you - I've always found an interesting tension in your writing. On the one hand you can be very scathing about, say, mysticism, but on the other hand there seems to be something more than just a sociological or detached, scholarly interest in the subject. There's a real sense of attraction, and even hints of belief...

IS: All those things are absolutes in my life. It's a turn that's got to be heard; it's very easy to drop off into these other aspects, where you're becoming a flaneur of the mystic, and I'm suspicious of it, but at root I'm really a big believer.

KJ: Can you be a bit more explicit?

IS: [Laughs.] It isn't like joining the Masons, there's not a set of rules that I sign up to, I just believe in the absolute life of the imagination, and the plurality of... everything.

KJ: The crunch question here would be: push comes to shove, are you a materialist or not?

IS: Not. Not at all, no. Far from. Though I have to enact being one for large chunks of my life. But by nature and temperament I'm absolutely one of those mad Welsh preachers who believes that... deliver the speech and you'll change someone's life. Or kill them. I really believe all that, but I can't go around spouting that and survive, so I'll adapt equally to the Scottish side of me, which is cynical, rational and cynical, and I believe in that as well.

KJ: So one side of your brain is David Hume...

IS: ... It's Stevenson, the classic Scottish Jekyll and Hyde thing. One is really deranged and manic, the other is looking at it being deranged and manic, and commenting on it. That's the tension. In the sixties, the balance was probably in the other way. I was actually standing back and looking slightly suspiciously at all this, while being attracted by certain elements within it. With the passage of time, in the next few years, which I think were the most important, I lost that cynical way of looking at it and went right into it, there were no handholds. I went right in.

I think that was the real breakthrough. It required this cataclysmic thing of the sixties, a sudden charge coming from every direction, a real battery. If things had worked out in terms of making these films, then that would have been a way in which life would have gone, but luckily it didn't. I pulled back, got into my own territory, created my own space and took things on my own terms. And that meant going out into a series of strange labouring jobs across the landscape of East London, and for the first time really getting an understanding of it from the dirt up. Things I would never have got otherwise - and I think all that was much more important to me than being at university.

KJ: Before we move on to that: what had happened between the end of making the Ginsberg film and the start of this time of casual labouring?

IS: We shot the Ginsberg film in the summer of 1967 and then went to Holland to edit it. After that, we looked in the newspaper one Saturday morning - *The Times*, of all places - and saw this ad that said you could have a house on the island of Gozo for three quid a week for the winter, while we were paying five quid a week for one room in Belsize Park. And I thought at that time, having done the Ginsberg film, that I could surely write some more documentaries, taking more time - this one was written in half an hour, in one afternoon, and we got to make it, so let's carry on with this!... and also I wanted to do a novel of the Irish material.

KJ: That anticipates a question I was going to ask: whether *White Chappell, Scarlet Tracings* was really your first novel?

IS: Probably the first completed novel... Obviously all the Irish matter was still fresh in my mind at that time. Anyway, we rented this house - it was from the man who represented Sooty's operative, Harry H. Corbett, his agent - we rented this house and took ourselves off to the Mediterranean. It was a very nice, stoneblock house on the edge of a village, with about a 20 minute walk down to the sea, so we went swimming every day. We were there in October, and stayed through winter. I started to write what would have been the first novel, an account of the Dublin years, very much in the form of the prose you were getting from Fielding Dawson or Robert Creeley - short, discursive, documentary lines edited by a nervous energy.

KJ: Not plot-driven?

IS: The book as a whole was plot-driven, but each of these segments would be independent, Polaroid portraits of a particular state in Dublin. As these amassed, they broke through into a more extreme form of fiction, so that there was a parallel narrative of a fabulous kind cut against a diary reality of Dublin, something like the material you get in *Kodak Mantra Diaries*, but also an extension of the same things, as though you'd pushed these same people into what would have been a novel.

KJ: How far did you get with it?

IS: I finished a first draft, and I was thinking that I'd go back to London and polish it up, but when I got back I picked up a copy of Tom Raworth's *A Serial Biography*, which had come out, and immediately I thought, "Right", chucked my manuscript in a case and never looked at it again, because it was the same format - exactly what I'd done, but in a much more polished and sophisticated way.

KJ: Do you think you'll ever dig it out?

IS: I don't know... it might be quite interesting to re-read just in terms of memories of Dublin, to see how I handled it. It was brought to a reasonable state of finish, would have required a bit of work to get it ready, and I would have done it through Albion Village Press, it wasn't going to be a big book - I suppose, about 120, 150 pages, a slender thing. But this Raworth book banged it on the head, because, as I say, he'd done exactly what I was trying to do and had done it much better, so, forget it...It couldn't have been sent off to Jonathan Cape to be offered as a novel, it wouldn't have fitted anywhere.

But while I was in Gozo, I also wrote quite a lot of film stuff, one of which was a more sophisticated version of the Ginsberg film, this time with Burroughs. I was in correspondence with him about this (and also with Graham Greene): it was a script in which he would have played himself. It wouldn't have been done in terms of head-on interviews, it would have been his material and enactments, a bit in the mood of those Anthony Balch films [such as *Towers Open Fire*]. He was up for it, but the Germans were hesitant, they didn't seem to have much of a market for Burroughs at that moment, and then he disappeared into Scientology anyway, so that drifted to nowhere. I guess the script still exists. It took the form of an interrogation - motifs that then engendered cutting, so that you were into two-screen things, and there was a man with a drill, who drills a lightbulb which explodes - he was a kind of Doctor Benway figure. I think it would have been better than the Ginsberg film, except that the Ginsberg film contains interest now as a historical snapshot of the period.

KJ: Has the Ginsberg film ever been shown in England?

IS: I sold it to the BBC at the time. This was when Jonthan Miller's *Monitor* was on the air. So I went over there and re-edited it with a BBC editor, and then they decided not to show it in toto but pillaged sections of it which you still see from time to time - Hyde Park and the dope rally appears regularly, bits of Stokeley Carmichael... but a video was made in Holland which you could buy, and is still around, and a couple of years back it appeared at the Rotterdam Film Festival when Chris Petit and I were over there showing *The Falconer*. It's a period piece, nice colour.

And the other main film project I did was - back to Vernon Watkins and this Welsh business - I took his verse play *The Ballad of the Mari Lwyd* and I wrote quite a worked-out structure of how you'd handle that [laughs], ostensibly with the weird idea that... well, Richard Burton at that time had joined the board of HTV and there was a big cultural push. And the TV company in Cardiff responded very positively, and I was invited down there. So I went to this man's office, and he said, "Fine, we'll do it, what budget would you like?" I thought, well, I don't want anything to do with ctors, I just wanted to hand it over to somebody and see the back of it, so I chickened out of that one altogether. Which is a pity in some ways, because I would have really liked to work with that material of Vernon Watkins, it was a myth that was very close, about dead returning on New Year's Eve.

My mother's family had been the keepers of this horse's head, the legend the play is based on, this shamanic horse's head called the Mari Lwyd. There's a village nearby Maesteg called Llan - which just means a church on a hill - and in that village there's one particular family who had the duty of looking after the horse's head and bringing it out on New Year's Eve, and then these people would go from house to house singing, and if you couldn't reply in verse, you had to let them in and give them drink and food, and if you could reply you kept them out. And I can remember them coming to our house, and I saw this horse's head in the cottage - it's now in the National Folk Museum, I think... I think an element of that still survives in Wales, though it's horribly swallowed up in the Dylan Thomas industry.. You can't move through marine South Wales now without encountering something like "The Dylan Thomas Suite" in the St David's Hotel in Cardiff - a suite in which Euro-businessmen hold breakfast bullshit sessions. It's everywhere. In Swansea docks there's an entirely bogus statue of Dylan Thomas, and his actual writing shed has been bought and stuck into a museum... horrible.

But there's a real side of it - a mythology that Ceri Richards painted, and Vernon Watkins was going on about, and for me all that was running in parallel with the Beats. So...there I was, being in Gozo and writing, on the one hand, a Burroughs script and, on the other hand, this Vernon Watkins thing, and Vernon Watkins died while we were living there. After his years as a bank clerk he finally got some measure of freedom and went to teach in America, Seattle, I think, he was playing tennis, had a heart attack and dropped dead.

But the period of being on Gozo was a very important one for us, and I really liked that kind of freedom, sunshine and sea. The food was terrible, but we grew stuff, and the people in the village brought gifts round - on Christmas Eve they brought Anna a kicking bag - it was a chicken, a live chicken, and they fell about laughing when she said she couldn't kill it, they cackled. And then they took it away and came back about ten minutes later with this horrible warm, bloody thing. We cooked it for hours. It was totally inedible.

KJ: The title of your early collection *Muscat's Würm* [1972] also comes from Gozo, doesn't it?

IS: When you landed in Malta very early in the morning, you used to be taken to the Grand Harbour. People who had just flown in from England were given a free breakfast on this terrace. The light was stunning. Then you got on this battered old bus and you drove right across the island to get the ferry, and in the course of this journey we passed a bar, with wonderfully primitive paintings on

in colour, a mixture of diary reality and myth. Strange, primitive things, but I enjoyed doing them and, as I say, showed quite a few in the Whitechapel exhibition. Some were bought by Ray Cooper, a percussionist who played with Elton John... and then, as I say, there were these photographs I'd taken.

KJ: Were you consciously trying to develop an idiosyncratic visual style for these photographs, or were they more in the nature of note-taking?

IS: The photos were fairly classic, black-and-white, very much stright-on with not much egoic interference, not hyper-arty.. A standard landscape tradition without being rhetorical about it. They were relatively clean aesthetically, and not like the colour snapshots I was taking at the same time, which were much more like loggings, humorous and quirky and surreal.

KJ: Where did your interest in ley lines and related matters begin? With John Michell, like most people at that time?

IS: Yeah, John Michell, [Alfred] Watkins, all of that. But then with Elizabeth Gordon's book on London - because in all of this there was a spiritual, seeking dimension - not necessarily for me, but for the people I was associated with. I remember being with somebody in a bookshop in Buckingham Palace Road, some strange little outlet, and the woman in there said "You should read this", and gave me *Prehistoric London: Its Mounds and Circles* by Elizabeth Gordon. And I thought, ooh, this is a real beauty. This is exactly what I wanted, because it lined up sacred spots of geography in London, and I thought, this definitely applies to what I know - like the Hawksmoor churches....

KJ: And the background to these esoteric studies is a sense of self-reliance, of complete carefreeness about what the rest of the world considers important...

IS: It was a privilege of that sixties era. Everything felt very comfortable, there was no fright about getting employment. No one I knew had any ambition to be this or that, or to have any kind of career, or even to get Jonathan Cape to publish them. It just did not enter your head... And also, there was a whole world of underground activity - publishing, magazines that came through regularly and kept you informed of what was happening in America, there were readings all the time. I mean, there was this culture, wasn't there? I'm not inventing it... there were bookshops like Compendium, or Indica before it, there would always be a book-shop that would take your stuff, you had a small outlet into the world, you weren't some demented sect lost in the backwoods. And I think those first years of the seventies were the best for it, because so much of the sixties had been taken up with psychedelic gangsters and chancers, Notting Hill people with private money tarting around.. And that had got burnt off a bit, you had to be serious to be carrying on. By the early seventies people like Bill Griffiths were producing their own books, Allen Fisher, Eric Mottram was organ-ising readings...

KJ: Was there a sense of a kind of dispersed community of like-minded writers?

IS: Yes, and in the early seventies I began to discover this commu-nity. There was one bunch, obviously, based on Cambridge, there was a London group under the patronage of Eric Mottram, with Bob Cobbing, who'd been a figure in Jeff Nuttall's *Bomb Culture*... this lot took over the Poetry Society in Earl's Court, so there was a venue there, there were presses there to be used, Bob Cobbing had his own presses... there was a degree of interchange, people who didn't know each other would meet at readings and give readings together - that was happening all the time. So it didn't matter what you were doing in your day-to-day life - I think Allen Fisher was a salesman of plastic pipes, Bill Griffiths was being a Hell's Angel. Barry McSweeney was in the Maritime Museum in Greenwich -

and yet here were these texts and you realised that people were doing extraordinary things.

KJ: Tell me a little more about the details of the labouring jobs. You mentioned that Catling joined you in some of these jobs..

IS: It was Catling who got me the job in Truman's Brewery. It was a classic job to get, and he'd got it, and said that there was a vacancy, so I went in after him, and then, later, got him recruited into cutting the grass in Limehouse. So we've shovelled a lot of dogshit together, and tipped a lot of ullage in cellars..

The era when we were working together in Truman's was magic. This area of Brick Lane still had the ambience of the Late Victorian era, a derelict area with the Brewery as its focus. You could do your day's work, and then you were out into the streets by 10 o'clock in the morning. You'd start at about 6.30, 7.00 - a pint of porter on the desk as you came in, and a sponsored breakfast in the canteen. Then you had a couple of lorries to deal with - quite hard physical graft, tipping the ullage away - and then you were done, took off, came back to have some lunch and then went to sleep in a hammock. The great thing was that we were able to explore this landscape, which fed back into my novel, *White Chappell*, crime, Gothic - it was all there.

And this was the era when I experienced a series of auditory hallucinations of one sort or another. The first and strangest thing that happened was that, during one of our walks, as we came onto Vallance Road, there was a little terrace of cottages, and an old Jewish guy used to sit outside them on his rocking chair, by himself, still wearing his pyjamas. Every day, we'd pass by him, and one day, after one of these brewery lunches, we wandered down there and noticed an agit-prop poster about social services, in which they'd changed the initials of social services into an SS flash. So Catling went into a sort of cod-German rant, Erich von Stroheim, alongside this old man, and he just panicked, he went into a rictus of terror and vanished into his house...

71

KJ: A camp survivor?

IS: That's the possibility, something of that ilk. He had bright dyed red hair, and always wore his pyjama tops covering his arms so you couldn't see if there were any tattoos... anyway, the pattern of the day was that there'd be some drinking, supper at my house, and we'd fall asleep on the floor. We were doing this, and the TV news came on, and there was this story, and I saw this Jewish guy's face on the screen. His name was Hymie Beaker, and he'd been savagely beaten in some kind of racist attack - because there was a lot of National Front activity in Whitechapel at that time, with the Bangladeshis coming in - and he was in the London Hospital. And they said, the suspect is - and a photo-fit picture of the suspect appeared on the screen, and it was like this terrible hybrid of Catling and myself squeezed together! Some third being had got away - this was the kind of drunken, nightmare aspect of it - this Jekyll-and-Hydish thing: from two people wandering through the area, a third being of some terrible malignancy was released, and starts committing crimes...

KJ: Is that what occultists call a *tulpa*?

IS: If you're going to be Tibetan about it, yes, that would be it... I mention this episode in *White Chappell, Scarlet Tracings.* Anyway, after that, there were a number of very strange things, auditory hallucinations. One of them was in the Whitechapel Gallery. The building was locked, we were there setting up the Albion Village exhibition and there was nobody else there, and this voice - like Ginsberg describing the voice of Blake coming to him in New York - this voice came out of somewhere and said: "Ramsey holds the Key." So we drove up to Ramsey Church in Huntingdon, but I couldn't find anything that was related to this voice. The name "Ramsay" (Michael Ramsay, Chevalier Ramsay) crops up in various occult circles - a figure connected with the Scottish Masons...

KJ:... back to our starting point...

72

IS: So I never discovered what "Ramsey holds the Key" meant at that time. But we carried on doing these journeys, based on rings radiating out from Ramsey Church, and finally ended up in Borley Rectory. [*At one time notorious as "the most haunted house in England", and much investigated by the then-famous psychic investigator Harry Price*], which was much more Catling's obsession than mine, he was very interested in Harry Price - an obsession which eventually led to a film he made about a talking mongoose. So we went to Borley, and took a tape recorder - because I think that the site where the Rectory stood there's not very much to see, it's gone - but the church was chilling, and we recorded some curious sound in there, very difficult to describe, not *Stone Tapes* stuff, not groaning.

It played against an episode in St Anne's Limehouse. I was approached by a man called Paul Green, a poet and writer, who had set up to record three radio programmes for the BBC's religious affairs department, based on three poets - Lee Harwood, Allen Fisher and myself, and this was to be the first one in the series. Paul Green had picked up on the fact that there was a poetic of place: Allen Fisher had done this large book called *Place*, which was an Olsonian epic about South London, and Lee Harwood had written about Brick Lane, very well, in the sixties. So we went with a BBC crew down to St Anne's, and at that time the crypt was still full of bones and bodies, it was like crawling around in the bottom of a pyramid with candles and torches. So we were fitted up with directional mikes, and we did an interview in the body of the church, upstairs, and we did one on the stairs, and it was all going absolutely fine, and then we crawled into the crypt and were describing what we could see, as if we were Howard Carter. It was pretty amazing, and I thought, "This is really great", and we came back upstairs after we'd done this stuff, played the tape back and there was nothing there. The tape was just full of this strange breathing: *hhhhhuuuuhhhh ... hhhhhhuuuuhhhh....*

And this was attemped three times, until the sound recordist said, "I'm not doing any more of this..."

KJ: He was spooked?

IS: He was completely spooked, because otherwise the thing was working perfectly. And even at the bottom of the stairs, I would speak some standard Hawksmoor babble and he could record it, but the minute we went in, and started crawling through and describing, there was nothing except this strange breathing.

KJ: Well, to play the rationalist, I suppose you could account for the lack of signal by the barrier of stones..

IS: But it wasn't that there was *nothing* - there was this definite sound, like a slow-motion breathing, or gasping.

KJ: So were you spooked?

IS: Not that spooked, because the place itself was so strange this was a by-product... not long after that the crypt was cleaned out and turned into a day centre. The BBC never broadcast the programme, which just exists as a pirated tape. They thought this was too sinister, it's not religion, it's not poetry, we're not going to have it.

So, in this period, it was as if the landscape was breaking up like an ice floe, and there were voices still registering, there were manifestations that weren't subsequently available...because it all too soon disappeared, under serious development. It was as if this was exactly the right moment to go into this quarter, it was still there. Active, available.

KJ: But this period was the only time that you ever had what might be classified, however loosely, as an occult experience?

IS: Oh no, no... There were lots of others. [*Laughter*] But this was really a highlight. The point is that they were not really occult experiences, they were everyday experiences within that climate, and that climate no longer exists. We both, separately, Catling and I, drew things from it, which he uses in his current work - a lot of stuff about possession, mediumship, tapping... all those things, and he's developed these techniques for going into places and sounding out what would be the voices or resonances within that place. And, by different means, that's what I've tried to do through writing. The material that's sometimes called "psychogeography" is loosely based on that era of primitively sounding out place through possession or seance, rather than... trying to summon entities, to communicate with them or control them. It wasn't that at all. It was as if certain places released voices... more than anything visual, there were no visual hallucinations. And that was interesting for me, because all the films I was making at the time were resolutely silent, pure Brakhage cinema, there was never a sound-track, I never made any sound recordings...

KJ: For the benefit of future compilers of the *Oxford English Dictionary*, maybe we'd better have the Sinclair definition of what that slippery word "psychogeography" means.

IS: I think the word first crossed my path in the 1960s, but it didn't really take. The Situationist Era drifted through me, and I didn't think I was practising anything which resembled it, until it kicked in as a term employed by Stewart Home and his associates, who were re-working cultural history, and using Situationist terms to parody the National Front's activities in Limehouse. I mean, they weren't seriously interested in where things fell on the map, they were just using those forms, but I seriously *was* interested in where things fell on the map. I thought psychogeography could be adapted quite conveniently to forge a franchise - which is what happened, more than I could have imagined! [Laughs] It took off!

I think of it, I suppose, as a *psychotic* geography - stalking the city. That's it, really. You need a bit more bite in the term than the whole ley-line thing which is...

KJ: A bit soggy?

IS: A bit soggy... a church tower here, a landmark there - I wanted it to include *everything*. Patterns and lines and ways of moving...

KJ: It's more than a metaphor for you?

IS: It's more than a metaphor.

KJ: But at the heart of it is the belief that something which happens in a place permanently affects that place?

IS: Very much so. There are these acoustic chambers in the city, voices and echoes...

[*There follows a digression on why Sinclair shuns Cambridge so rigorously these days, which then segues back to the Catling theme.*]

KJ: Isn't there a photograph of you and Catling dressed in Victorian clothes?

IS: Well, he is. This was outside Hymie Beaker's house... I was just dressed in what everyone was wearing at the time, but Catling - he denies he ever dressed like this, but he did - he used to go around dressed like Sherlock Holmes, in a stiff collar, a tie, a formal suit of some kind, and his room in Camberwell, which I filmed, so I can prove it, was actually like a pastiche of 221b Baker Street, full of clay pipes and pistols and books of reference, lots of little drawings and objects... It was a beautiful house, a Victorian house, quite large, and his adoptive parents lived in the upper half so that he had the whole ground floor and basement to himself. So he dressed like that, and he had all this weird kit, it was uncanny. He had no money to speak of, it was all scavenged from gutters and street markets, he'd go to the Kingsland Road market on Saturdays and find stuff.

KJ: Was he completely self-invented, or were his parents also pasticheurs?

IS: Not at all, they were a very pleasant Camberwell couple who had adopted this child, and I feel he was completely self-invented. For whatever reason, he had taken on this persona... He was saturated in writers like Poe - I remember he had a wonderful edition of "The Raven" which he showed me - and he obviously read a lot of H.P.Lovecraft, and he lived in the past, in the sense that he visted a lot of museums.

KJ: I assume that even when he was officially your student, the relationship was never one of master to pupil..

IS: No, not at all. I mean, all I could usefully do was throw a lot of writers who I thought might be useful at him, and some of them took, and some of them didn't. I know that for example, showing him Beckett's *Poems in English* was a major breakthrough for him, because the language, some of the formal twists and stringiness of the Beckettian language, was very important for him, it just devoured him. Whereas trying to give him Olson was a total waste of time, none of that took in the slightest. So I suppose I was useful to him in the sense of being able to offer him certain possiblities that otherwise would not have come his way... and also, more importantly I suppose, published his first four books through Albion Village Press.

KJ: I don't know them. *Necropathia* is the first, isn't it? What's it like?

IS: It's interesting. A mixture of what I've been describing to you in terms of English Gothic - murders and brown rooms and dirt... also a kind of refracted, cinematic Gothic of asylums - machines and skull-faced madmen. But on a secondary level, there's a very strong sense of English landscape, he was keen on Wiltshire and Dorset and the Ridgeway - a sense of being out there in cottages.... very much in his own voice. But the weirdest thing that happened with the first book - again, this happened at the time of the exhibition at the Whitechapel Gallery - was that the book had a lot of photographs in it of a faked, sado-masochistic kind, a pastiche of *News of the World* stories, that dark English side. And there were also some photographs from a text book of murder, about some person who had hanged themseleves in Epping Forest dressed as a woman... So I got a call from some lawyers in Leeds one day, saying, are you the publisher of *Necropathia*? Can you send us some of your other books? Because I think they thought they'd stumbled on some major pornographer... All the other Albion Village books were Chris Torrance's poems about birds and bees, and my London ramblings! [*Laughter*] Anyway, it turned out that somebody in Leeds had commited this appalling murder, and when they searched his house they found a copy of *Necropathia*, which they felt might have influenced him. It became a centre spread in *The Sun* at the time, while we were in the Gallery. We came outside and there was a news-stand selling the *Sun*, and this huge spread, "Horror Book Found in Murder Case" - "an atrocious book, in appalling print" - which I liked -

KJ: Was there any reciprocal influence of Catling on you at that time?

IS: In a sense, yes. Because he'd lived in London all his life, and his heritage of the Old Kent Road pubs, and business that went on under arches, and the ghosts of Whitechapel... he'd known all that since he was a kid, and it was of a very different order from me coming in as a 20-odd year old, discovering it. So I got a very different sense of London from knowing him.

KJ: Am I right in remembering that you had a bit of a respite from then labouring scene, and went to the Coutauld Institute for a while?

IS: Well, as I said, for my degree in Dublin I'd done a course in European art and enjoyed it, and thought subsequently when I was doing one of my labouring jobs - I think out in Stratford, loading and unloading containers - that it would be quite nice to come indoors out of the weather for the winter. And one of the possiblities I'd looked into earlier was going on to do a postgraduate art degree of some sort, and there wasn't a lot of choice then, so the obvious slot was the Courtauld Institute. So I went there, got interviewed by a man called Alan Bowness, a successful art politician - who went on to the Old Tate, I think... And signed on, to do an MA for a couple of years, without really knowing what the place was. And it was so utterly bizarre, having come from this world of labouring in East London which I'd been doing for a couple of years... This was in, what, 1972, 73.. And I couldn't really afford to be there anyway, because you couldn't get a grant the second time around, so essentially it was never going to work.

But more importantly I found at that point I could not write the required essays. They were just wrong. Ten years before it would have been water off a duck's back, but now I was into doing other things. So I was only there for a term or so. And it was fine, I enjoyed aspects of it. People like John Golding were very good, good stuff on Cubism, good lectures on Cézanne, and you'd just sit there and very happily look at slides, listen to the voices droning on... wonderfully restful. And I also at the same time started to explore parts of West London, around Manchester Sqaure, and spent a lot of time in the ethnographic sections of the British Museum - that fixated me.. And I wrote a book of poems, *The Birth Rug*, that incorporated Cézanne material with tribal art and material from my afternoons there.

KJ: Did you ever write any straight essays?

IS: No, I wrote this book of poems in lieu. But what I hadn't appreciated was the intrinsic weirdness of the Courtauld Institute, and its central focus in the alternative history of British culture...

KJ: Sir Anthony Blunt...

IS: Blunt is there, living up above the place with his spy-masters coming in and out to interrogate him, with gay rent-boys coming in, louche parties upstairs... Anita Brookner was elsewhere with her minimalist, pointilliste little novels...I mean, a whole chunk of stuff which went on which I hadn't even recognised, because the whole tone of it was very Sloane-y, well-connected ladies, probably moving on to Sotheby's, and creatures like Brian Sewell, with accents beyond accents. And then there were one or two low-lifers like me who drifted in, most of whom fell off for various reasons...

KJ: Were you an exact contemporary of Brian Sewell's?

IS: Oh no, he was gone long before me... but I remember vividly when the Blunt case broke, Sewell appearing on TV to defend him, with this strangulated voice, which probably launched his media career.

KJ: Brian Sewell once appeared in a documentary film I was involved in making, about Poussin, and Blunt's Poussin scholarship, and I remember him saying that one of Blunt's indisputable achievements was that he had turned the Coutauld from a sort of unofficial finishing school for upper-class girls, and gave it some real intellectual rigour.

IS: Yes, I think that's true. He made connections with the Warburg Institute, which was definitely more rigorous, and it was certainly more than a finishing school by the time I got there, though there was still an element of that... waiting for a husband thing, or gay thing, or wanting to use art as an alternative to a dirtier career. But it was changing to something much more technical, more professional.

KJ: I assume that you'd feel more of a natural affinity with the Warburg style - Dame Frances Yates, theatres of memory, occult and pagan traditions...

IS: Oh God, yes. Oh yes, obviously. I would have jumped at all that, it just never occured to me at the time that it was even an option. But I was reading Frances Yates, all the John Dee and Queen Elizabeth material.. The Coutauld didn't touch that stuff. The Courtauld was to do with looking at a painting, breaking the painting down square by sqaure.. And every single inch of the painting would refer back to another painting, and all you had to do was discover these genealogies and list them. It was art through the wrong end of the telescope, and of minimal interest from that point of view, but it was very provocative just to sit in the dark and look at slides for hours at a time. I loved it. If could have stayed for two years just writing poems and having this as one intravenous drip of

81

culture I would have done it... if I'd had any money. But I didn't, it was madness, so I passed on... not knowing of David Rodinsky's fascination with the area... one of the most mysterious of Rodinsky's A-Z maps was this red line that he dots out from East London.. It wanders about, and then comes right past the Courtauld Institute, then past the Wallace Collection in Manchester Square, and finishes up in Regent's Park. Why he made that particular detour I'll never know. It would be nice to think he knew Anthony Blunt. Because the one significant object which survived in Rodinsky's room was this calendar picture of Millet's "Angelus"... It would be nice to think he did a deconstruction with Anthony Blunt. All human life passed through there one way or another.

KJ: Did you ever see Frances Yates lecture?

IS: No, I just read the books... and not long after this period, of course, all this other, alternative Poussin reading started to kick in with *The Holy Blood and the Holy Grail*, so I was hearing those things from the start. And Blunt's scholarship on Poussin was being called into question, there were serious challenges about some of his attributions...so this was a strange interlude for me, but I realised very soon I couldn't carry it on. I remember walking up to Stoke Newington, sitting down in Abney Park Cemetery one afternoon, and thinking, it's been good fun, but I'm going to have to put this one behind me, and go back out to Hackney Marshes. So that's what happened.

[*Here followed a digression on Occulist and Satanist activities in Abney Park, which led to the apparent non-sequitur:*]

KJ: Were you ever on the fringe of any occult groups in the way you were on the fringe of political groups?

IS: No... I never had any dealings with that. And obviously if I had, I wouldn't say. The only practicing magicians I've ever come across are Alan Moore and Peter Whitehead.

KJ. And that's another story... Still on the theme of the visual arts, when did your interest in photography start to take shape?

IS: All along. I started taking photographs at an early age, 10, 12 or so, always had a camera, and when I moved to London, came to film school, we were told to get out on the streets with cameras, do that Parisian number, carry it around with you at all times. So I got into the habit of taking a camera with me, took thousands of pictures of South London streets, congregational churches, markets, pollarded suburban trees... And it carried on into Dublin.

KJ: It's clear from some of your asides in *Lights Out* and elsewhere that you do know at least a fair amount about the history of photography. Knowledge picked up on the hoof, or deliberate study?

IS: I've always been keenly interested in people like Robert Frank. In a sense, I come to him through Kerouac, but then went on to be very interested both in him and in that type of photography. Photography has been a very important element in how I write... and before that, painting as well. I wasn't under pressure to produce huge swathes of prose, so that, as well as a short prose pieces or a poem, I would always log a visual image alongside it. And sometimes, from the photographs I would make paintings, as a sort of device for taking something to another place... So I'd jump about between the three things, painting, photography and writing.

KJ: And, just to spell it out, taking lots of photographs is still an important part of your working method?

IS: Taking photographs is still a major resource for memory, structure... particularly with things like *London Orbital*, where every journey is just hundreds of photographs, which saves me from writing down notes. I'd rather have the images.

KJ: Back to some literary markers. When did you first pick up on J.H. Prynne?

IS: In the early seventies. I used to go to Compendium a lot. At one time they expanded to a whole shop of poetry, and there was Prynne on the shelf. I wanted to call my own first book *Kitchen Poems*, that was the title I'd picked, because at the time we had a room at the top of the house - it's my daughter's bedroom now - which was a kitchen with a kind of New York metal staircase which went down to the garden, and we spent a lot of time sitting in the sunlight of this kitchen cooking up endless dishes of rice, drinking coffee and talking, and I thought the title of *Kitchen Poems* was perfect for this first book, and I was really pissed off to see that someone else had beaten me to it. I picked it up and it looked very Olsonian, the whole set-up looked like the *Maximus* poems. I thought, I'm not sure about this, but shortly afterwards I found *The White Stones* in a bookshop in Primrose Hill, and I was knocked out by it: amazing! And at the same time this guy called Chris Bamford, who's been the one I'd written my two plays with in Dublin, a very old friend, had just come back from America and said, the ultimate message, the real man we've got to go see, is this man Prynne.

So he managed to find out that Prynne was in Caius College, Cambridge, rang him up and Prynne said, "Yeah, OK, you can come up and see me one afternoon." So we went up there, and the pitch we were making to him at the time was that I was really convinced that we could set up a sort of Black Mountain School in England and he could be the Rector. [Laughs] So we came with this bizarre notion, pitched it to him, and he was very genial and affable, and what he said lasted much longer for me than what Ginsberg had said. Extraordinary vistas were opened up by a long, long afternoon's conversation. We parted, and I remember it was agreed that Chris would immediately initiate a correspondence with Prynne and it would lead towards some sort of possibility of setting this thing up. And then Chris disappeared back to America immediately [laughs], and never wrote a letter at all, but did in fact set up something quite similar in America - he lived with the Lindisfarne community for a while - it wasn't his creation, but he got into it, and they invited people like Kathleen Raine and [Gregory] Bateson to live there, they had a press, and they were into things like Critchlow and sacred measurement. So I think that the conversation with Prynne was very important to him, but it led him to form his own ideas. And to me it was very important, in that I got a rigorous sense of what the ethical responsibilities of this new poetic could be, and the excitment of the dazzling intelligence there, available.

KJ: Could you spell out what you mean by ethical responsibilities?

IS: Oh, just being a poet - the care with which you have to choose the words you're using. It can't be throwaway - it can be loose, free, but at some level you've got to take a real responsibility, and it matters a lot whether you stop this word there or *there*... You really had to think about it in a way I hadn't done before. Some time later Prynne called by in Albion Drive, and we spent a long night in conversation, and looking at the films I'd made, and again, I thought there was stuff here I could chew on for a very long time. That was major.

KJ: Tell me a little more about these films.

IS: They were called "Diaries", and set out simply to map and log the lives that were being lived in this Hackney community, but as time went on they pitched into more fictional or else lyrical forms. Tom Baker's tended towards landscape lyricism, with a lot of multiple superimposition. Looking back on them now, the things that interest me most are just the loggings of place. It's amazing to see the people and what it all looked like, and the less messed-up the better. But it developed two strategies, one of which was lots of single-frame shooting, so that three minutes of film would be months of time, and everything was notated, you could notate very fast. The other was superimposition, so I might cover one part of the lens with a finger, and have one side un-superimposed, and the other superimposed, so you never knew quite what you were going to get... but the density of these images was astonishing. Ten hours of this would represent miles and miles of a life, everything included.

KJ: You still have this?

IS: It's all been transferred onto tape. In the film *London Orbital* there are images from those films - Anna is there... There's an enormous archive of that time which we'll probably be tapping into... Talking now, in retrospect, it might look as if it was all planned, but it was just a day to day sense of, we're here, this is great, let's do this, let's do that, we'll do that tomorrow.. It all happened randomly and accidentally. Until, after 1975, things changed quite dramatically.

KJ: What happened around 1975?

IS: Suddenly and noticeably it became harsher as an environment, moving towards the beginning of that Thatcher period which was on the horizon.

KJ: Up until that time, which is also the time of *Lud Heat*, you'd been working almost excusively on a small, even a miniature scale, with lyrics and chapbooks. Was that just economic necessity, or was it also the nature of your project at the time?

IS: I'd come down to small scale, because I started on mock-epic forms, like the huge *Waste Land* collage poem at film school, and I'd written some things in Dublin which were on a large scale, and I weeded all that out. Cut, cut, cut, till I was happiest with these small, fragmentary forms. That seemed to suit the pace of the life. Film-making was exactly the same: single frame, just click click click click.. Getting everything down in a very sharp way. Writing and film were part of the same thing.

KJ: Was it experimental work, in the sense that you were doing it to discover how it would look?

IS: No, it just seemed like the simplest solution, nothing more. Wanting to do something very direct instead of this original, apocalyptic, mythological Celtic material. I wanted to move away from that, to a more narrative base, a sense of a man in the world, and what happens in this room, it's all right in front of your nose. And then I moved back from that, later, into the London mythology.

KJ: Apart from your brief stint at the Coutauld, did you always work as a manual labourer in these years, or was there a period where you went in for something more in the white-collar line?

IS: Well, there was one really extraordinary time, which happened when I'd just made a preliminary attempt to get into the Parks Department, before the job I had in Limehouse which led to the writing of *Lud Heat*. I was out on Hackney Marshes, where the job was marking out the white lines for the football pitches that were laid on top of the bomb damage from the Second World War, the rubble of East London. And I came back to Hackney one evening, and there was a large Rolls-Royce, a blue Corniche, outside my house, which was amazing, because in those days there weren't very many cars around Hackney. And Anna had let in this couple, who'd turned up on the doorstep and insisted that they must wait to see me. They were sitting in my room, looking at books, and when I came in the man just barked at me "Are you interested in John Cowper Powys?" Well, yes, reasonably... It turned out to be a man called Jeff Kwinter, who'd grown up in Hackney, educated himself through Mare Street public library, where Henry Miller had led him on to Powys, and he'd become obsessed by Powys. He had now become very wealthy, with a chain of clothes shops called Village Gate, and had the vision or instinct that he should found a press and acquire a book-shop. So his flagship property on Regent Street was going to be made over into Village Gate Bookshop, and he said, "You must be on the payroll. Turn up tomorrow to our office in King's Road, and consider yourself on the firm."

So I went down there the next day, and there was this whole bunch of people assembled - dowsers, ley line freaks, jugglers, acupuncturists, nutters and visionaries of every kind, thronging this office, who were going to re-invent the culture. And I was immediately told to get out of the rags I was wearing, given a suit from his shop and a tape recorder and the keys to a red Ferrari. I went home to Hackney, and was then shipped off to Wales to chase up John Cowper Powys's final mistress, and attend to the story. But by the time I got back to London, this guy said, "Oh, no, no, we're finished with that, we're moving on to the next thing. Off you go to Avebury and Stonehenge, take some photos, come on, keep moving." Everything was like that, Zen mastery and general all-purpose weirdness. One of the other people who was brought in had been working for Dunn's hatters. Jeff had said, "I can see you've got the vision", and gave him a suitcase full of books by John Cowper Powys and a ticket to New York, shoved him on the plane. One-way ticket. That was it. He was never seen again! [Laughs]

Anyway, as I say, the second project after the Powys search in North Wales was to go out and photograph sacred sites. So I went all over the place, and took photographs which were then exhibited in his shop, his gallery in Regent's Street - Avebury, Silbury, Stonehenge, the Ridgeway and all the rest of it, black and white, blown up, as part of this New Age set-up...

All this carried on for about six months. It was an amazing bookshop, where everybody turned up. Ted Hughes walked in and started buying books on Red Indian shamanism and ritual, Kenneth Patchen's wife Miriam turned up... and so it went on. I introduced a few other people into the scheme of things, and then one day I was taken with Brian Catling, who had a very bad stammer at that point, and we were locked into this office on King's Road with bottles of champange, to write - in half an hour! - exactly where the spiritual identity of Britain was at that moment in time. A motor-bike rider was waiting for this piece...I've got this photograph of Brian, who's got all his fingers in his mouth, chewing them to the bone, while he's sitting on the floor in the corner, unable to write a word, while I'm hammering out something on the typewriter...

That was a deranged period of time, we cruised around town in this Rolls-Royce with Kwintner and his house poet, Hugo Manning, pipe and duffle coat, going to the Sherlock Holmes pub... an element of all that creeps into *Suicide Bridge*, you'll see that one section of that is set in a bookshop where the magus flips open the *I Ching*, or Pound's *Cantos* or something, to see whatever gnomic message it delivers, and the day is set by that. So this whole thing of mad high commerce and visionary art was imposed on me right then, but with a secondary sense that it was all a game, it will never be real, but enjoy the ride while you're on it, and react to it. So by the time I met Mike Goldmark, who'd also been in this fashion world - Mr Kipper Ties, he'd become a millionaire on kipper ties, and lost it all, went bankrupt and ended up barefoot in Uppingham, selling double-glazing - I knew where we were at. When it came to publishing *White Chappell* I was more relaxed, but the first time was unworkable, the known world was taken apart and we were left floating. Fish out of water.

★★★

PART FOUR:

LUD HEAT TO *WHITE CHAPPELL,*
SCARLET TRACINGS

KJ: When did you first have a sense that the London mythology material was going to become a long-term project?

IS: I suppose the first inklings came in the late sixties, with all those books about earth mysteries, theories about Silbury Hill and the stones of Cornwall. That was when I started to get away from London and do quite long walks along these sacred paths of England - the sort of stuff Renchi was doing in later years.

KJ: Ley-line stuff?

IS: Not really ley lines, just a sense of pilgrim routes. If you start on the Ridgeway at Streatley, by the Thames, and walk down to Avebury - it's a nice couple of days out in the country, but it's also very resonant, you move through a particular landscape. You're not following a ley-line, but you are looking for something that's fairly grand in its matter. So we were doing a lot of that a long time before I applied the same principles to London. What was in my head originally was much more to do with the countryside.

KJ: As far as I know, the Hawksmoor proposition is original to you...

IS: I don't know... well, yeah, I think the notion of the relationship of the churches, the lines and patterns - I don't think I'd ever seen that written anywhere. I'm sure not.

KJ: Was there a *eureka* moment?

IS: Sort of. The most notable thing that struck me as I walked across this landscape for the first time were these run-down churches, and I suddenly realised, there's this one here and that one there, and maybe there is some connection. And then I did have this very vivid dream of St Anne's, Limehouse... and shortly afterwards, by accident or whatever, got this job from the Parks Department which sent me out to a place which was very close to the church, and I found myself cutting the grass near St Anne's, Limehouse. And prior to that I'd been up on the top of Greenwich hill and noticed that you could actually see, between the twin towers of the Naval College, exactly in the middle, St Anne's, Limehouse. This was before Docklands was built up.

And thinking of it in terms of those maps you used to see of London where the whole city was like a fleet which had come to rest, all the church towers... the city was marked out by church towers, that was the way the thing was organised, you had to belong to a church. So Nicholas Hawksmoor's churches - Christchurch, Spitalfields and St.Anne's, Limehouse and St. George-in-the-East - represented the suburbs - Wren represented the city, Hawksmoor's were outside the official nexus - and they were very significant. Also, they could be seen from the river, so they had a double register, as being outside London and forming a secondary energy source, and being what led you into London as you came up the river, when the river was still an active concern.

KJ: *Lud Heat*, the book in which you engage with these ideas, is more like an epic than anything you'd done for a long time...

IS: Yes... as I say, I did a book called *The Birth Rug*, which was the last of those domestic books, but which also made a lot of use of Sumerian material, which again would be very Olsonian, I suppose. I had a good correspondence with Jeremy Prynne around the time of that book, that was probably the point when I was most in active correspondence with him, and then after that I did a book which was never published, but which was finished, called *Red Eye*.

KJ: With some kind of Brakhage connection?

IS: Well, it was Brakhage domestic material. An equivalent to Brakhage's film cycle, his songs. I wanted to use lino cuts, very vivid colours and images, between each section, and the sections mixed this earlier mode of domestic recording with a real mapping of London, mostly based on St Pancras Old Church - which Aidan Dun subsequently took up [in *Vale Royal*]. I'd just wandered in there one day when I was working for the Post Office nearby, and I thought this was a numinous place... and of course there were all the connections between Shelley, Thomas Hardy and that burial ground. *Red Eye* also included material about Christchurch, Spital-fields, that Hawksmoor church, and sacred geometry. So that material was really rehearsed before *Lud Heat*, it's right on the edge of it, and then getting the gardening job which took me into this other landscape gave the whole thing. And even there, there's a combination of modes - diary perceptions of living and working as a gardener, and dealing with social, semi-political matters involved with that, and then the larger essays, which are epic, and are to do with the nature of the city on the grandest scale, from the beginning.

KJ: It's also, unless I've overlooked something, the first of your books in which comedy starts to poke its way up through the concrete...

IS: I think so. There are comic elements in the earlier stuff, but that's the first one in which there's a kind of rough and ready, real comedy.

KJ: There's a lot of Egyptological matter in *Lud Heat*, and you deploy Egyptian hieroglyphs quite freely. What was the extent of your Egyptological knowledge at the time?

IS: Oh, great interest, minimal knowledge. [Laughs]

KJ: Where did you swipe the hieroglyphs?

IS: I don't know... probably something I got from the British Museum. I used to hang around the British Museum and look at that stuff a lot. And also, the Pitt-Rivers, and the Horniman Museum - that was a beauty. So, those three places I'd go to quite often. It was also the period when people like Ed Sanders were writing Egyptian translations, there was a big interest in taking it back. His work was legitimate translation, but it was giving it an energy of the moment.

  Probably the two things that interested me most at the time were the way in which Ed Sanders was going, dealing with Charles

Manson and weird notions of apocalyptic cults in the desert, on the edge of Hollywood... and on the other hand, Ed Dorn's *Gunslinger* was coming through, this really speedy, clear, sharp vision of Howard Hughes.

KJ: *Lud Heat* now looks like a very significant book in your development. Did it feel that way at the time?

IS: Oh, it felt like it, yeah. It felt different, like I'd moved on to another stage.

KJ: Did it make much of a stir?

IS: Only very locally. It got out, in a way that none of the others had done... it was reviewed in the *Morning Star*! And people did begin to turn up on my doorstep. It definitely travelled around a circuit. A lot of people, I think, already had their own thoughts about the churches, and mappings of London, and were very intrigued by that. I think there were 500 copies offically done, probably about 600 or 700 really, and they went quite quickly, and that's without any real distribution, just through Compendium or people who ordered them from me. So that was a big moment... but then, after that, the whole thing collapsed. That world of small press publishing where you could have something that was a success on those terms, that couldn't happen any more.

KJ: So was *Lud Heat* the last of the Albion Village Press publications?

IS: No, no, in 1979 I published one called *Suicide Bridge*, which was done in parallel with *Lud Heat* - some of it was even started before it. It took longer to do. It was an attempt to re-animate a Blakean mythology, to do with the low life of East London. And there was a rap on Howard Hughes, which came out of Ed Dorn.

KJ: And it contains a digression to a certain place in east Anglia you can't stand.

IS: There's a digression to Cambridge... It's a place in which I've always felt uncomfortable for various reasons. It's obviously a deeply interesting place, but it's not somewhere I'm comfortable, that's all there is to it.

KJ: *Suicide Bridge* must surely be the first work of literature to pick up on the work of Stephen Hawking...

IS: Again, that's from Jeremy Prynne. What happened was that, through these conversations I had been having with Prynne, my whole notion of who the Illuminati of the culture were changed completely. I realised that at Caius College at one point there's been [Francis] Crick, Stephen Hawking, and Prynne. When I went to visit Prynne at one time there was a typsecript on his desk of Hawking's *Large Scale Structure of Space-Time,* which looked to me like an Egyptian manuscript, it was all hieroglyphics and symbols. Prynne was sort of translating this, working on it in some way... a poet doing this! The same person who had helped to edit and organise late Olson! I thought that this was very extraordinary, and realised that the worlds of science and literature were, at that point, engaged in an interesting dialogue, most of which was based on Cambridge. [Rupert] Sheldrake came along, with his mystical take on Morphic Resonance, which I enjoyed very much. [Laughs] He acknowledges Prynne as well, in his book. And Prynne got Crick in touch with Michael McClure, say, and there was a real area of sympathy between what Crick was working on at the time and the sort of poetic that McClure was exploring - psilocybin demons of animals. It was a very, very intriguing time.

KJ: The period of *Lud Heat* and *Suicide Bridge* seems on the one hand to close a phase in your writing, and on the other hand to initiate a new phase.

IS: I think that *Lud Heat*, *Suicide Bridge* and *White Chappell* are a kind of trilogy, and *White Chappell* is the end of that one and the beginning of another one. I felt that *Suicide Bridge* was, in the end, only half of what I'd intended, I'd wanted to go on and do a Part Two, but by the time I'd done it I thought it was a dead end... I was finished with it for the next few years. Partly because I was now plunged into book-dealing, but partly because it was all too heavy a project, it involved acres of time and research, and all sorts of broodings, and I just wanted to get out on the road. So the little things I did after that, for the next few years, were very throwaway and literally give-away.

KJ: From the late seventies until the late eighties, there's not a lot on the published record...

IS: No, there isn't. Three very small books - the first one, I think, was called *Fluxions*, the second was called *Flesh Eggs and Scalp Metal* - we used the title again later, for a different book - and the third was *Autistic Poses*. All knocked out from my desk-top in increasingly small editions. The first one was about twenty copies, the last one was down to about ten. I just gave them away, because I thought the audience for what I was doing had probably shrivelled to this number of people. There was no point, I didn't want to be involved, and I'd happily disappeared into the quasi-writing activity of being a book-dealer.

KJ: Do you look on that eight to ten years or so of minimal production as a lost period, a bad decade?

IS: No, as a very good one.... After *Lud Heat* I was already planning a prose book, but I said, I can't do it until I can have three months off, at least. And for some reason, I'd decided that I needed two thousand quid if I was going to write this book. And I never did have, between then and 1985 or whenever it was that I actually came to write *White Chappell*. I had the whole book in mind, I could have written one version of it in 1976 if I'd had the money, except that the more important part of the book, the deranged book-dealing aspect, wouldn't have been in it. All the other side of it was plotted, and actually delivered in various forms, in that interim period... including - at one time, I was going to do a reading with Brian Catling at London University or somewhere, and for some reason he was up in Norwich and because of trains or whatever he couldn't come, so I was faced with this solo thing...

I took the material I'd written, the Victorian fiction about the Ripper, with a lot of other material about silver, Peru, which was the other take at that time. A mad Texan millionaire called Bunker Hunt was cornering the world's silver markets and I got very interested in silver, and then in the South American aspects of silver, and this seemed to double up in a kind of alchemical way with what was going on in Whitechapel. So I created a whole novel with this material and then, literally, in a Burroughs way, cut it up, and chucked it in a hat, and read really the whole novel in these fragments. It worked really well. [Laughs.] I wish I'd kept it...it must be somewhere, but it was just a one-off. Probably Eric Mottram recorded it, because he recorded everything. So, if someone had said, "OK, here's two grand", I could have produced this book in 1977, 1978, which would have been in many ways quite similar. So when it finally arrived, in 1987, it was pretty thoroughly cooked, in advance. It just wrote itself.

Anyway, it wasn't a blank period for me, it was very interesting. It was really quite like the sixties thing, after the Dialectics of Liberation - discovering this underworld of book transactions, and travelling about - opening up England again, travelling all over the countryside and all over Europe, in very mad, speedy way. Huge amounts of information coming in, people coming up to you and telling you about lost books. All of that was there for a long time, and I thought, great! It's like a second education.

KJ: What was the content of that education?

IS: Well, it varied. Some of it was a sense of lost Victorian and Edwardian literatures - things which I'd only known in a vague way were made precise, figures like M.P. Shiel -

KJ: The first King of Redonda!

IS: Yes... and the backwaters of Gothic, of fin-de siecle literature. It came through meeting people, rather than any study. I learnt incalculable amounts from those secret scholars, the dealers and collectors - Martin Stone, Driffield, John Clute, John Eggeling, Donald Weeks, Gerry Goldstein, George Locke, Alan Clodd.

KJ: So: Arthur Machen?

IS: Machen, yeah...

KJ: Algernon Blackwood?

IS: No, he was one of Catling's enthusiasms. For me it was Shiel, Machen, William Hope Hodgson, Stevenson... I had a wrappered copy of *Strange Case of Dr Jekyll and Mr Hyde*... And then there were all the hard-boiled crime writers, Cornell Woolrich [William Irish] - not just Chandler and Hammett but David Goodis, Jim Thompson - all of that's pouring in.

KJ: I must admit that I find that stuff fairly unreadable, certainly not exciting...

IS: Oh? I do find it exciting... there's an interesting, end-of-the-tether feel. I've always been fond of pulp writing at its limits - it's hack-work, but so hack, so desperate, and they're drinking so much and their lives are so crazy, churning out these words, and I feel that a kind of mediumistic element happens, you kick into another level which separates it from the Mickey Spillanes, the complete journeymen who are just doing a job. Some of David Goodis, a lot of Jim Thompson is so psychotic that it's beyond genre. And that interests me. Ellroy had an element of it, too, when he started out.

KJ: And, to go to another genre, Philip K Dick -

IS: Yes, absolutely. But apart from all that, I remember someone coming round to me one day and saying, here, you should read this. And it was Frederick Treves' book about the Elephant Man. And this was very fruitful, way before any of the plays or the film or anything. And also, through book-dealing, I met a doctor - very often, doctors are book-collectors - and he took me into the London Hospital to see the Elephant Man's armature and cast... So I put all that into *White Chappell, Scarlet Tracings*, because that was going on at the same time as the Ripper murders. All that came through being a book-dealer, if I hadn't been a book-dealer I would never have met Joseph Sickert and got hold of the Gull material.

KJ: Was part of the interest in fin-de-siecle literature a sense that it was kind of a verbal counterpart to the East London cityscape you'd been exploring?

IS: There was a sense of it being a bit of a ghetto, an underground, a secret world not looked at much by academics, jewelled and strange... and there was a realisation that there were these huge tranches of literature that were outside the official canon, and how dull the official canon actually was... there were landscapes beyond belief that wouldn't have come my way if I hadn't been in that world, with people coming up to you and saying, you *must* read Gerald Kersh, so you go off and read *Fowlers End*, or *Night and the City*... or saying you must read *The Lowlife* by Alexander Baron. A lot of them turned out to be dull, but a lot of them stuck.

KJ: And how about *Dracula*? You eventually get round to addressing it directly in *London Orbital,* but I assume it was also part of the fin-de-siecle reading list.

IS: It was.. And... Oh, God! I still bleed about this - I found a superb first edition of *Dracula* in Bury St Edmund's in an Oxfam shop. Mint! The yellow cover, with red lettering - it looked like it had just been printed. It was 50 pence! And next to it was a crummy paperback which they'd priced up to one pound fifty, because it was a new paperback. So I bought it, and sold it soon after for a good price, about three hundred pounds, but today it would be worth thousands and thousands. You will never find it again, not in that condition. But those were the excitements of dealing. I didn't even dare to read the book, it was so beautiful.

KJ: But when you did read *Dracula*, you enjoyed it?

IS: Very much. All the different techniques, the typewriter technology, the recording devices... it's a bit clunky in lots of ways, but a rich source of many things... up until I came to write about Carfax Abbey at Purfleet, and the circulation of blood and oil...

KJ: I once had an argument with a Jungian analyst about *Dracula*, and said how sick to death I was of reading about how it is All About Sex, which seems to me about as interesting as saying that the James Bond books are all about espionage. The Bleeding Obvious. Whereas your take, that it's actually about real estate...

IS: It's fantastic on real estate, it's all about real estate right from the start, the moment he starts poring over these brochures of London. Dracula is the prime age of the Real Estate guy - that's what it's all about. All the rest is bad Victorian theatre, Henry Irving....

This second education was really a much more intense and rewarding one than the first, at Trinity Dublin. That was really a dozy time, and the best thing that came out of it was conversations at the pub, where other students would bring their enthusiasms to the table. The book-dealing world stepped that up twentyfold. With the added edge that if you didn't make a sale you didn't eat, you were on the cusp of survival. So there were all kinds of mad occult elements in that as well, in terms of... tricks, stunts that you would pull...

KJ: What do you mean?

IS: Well... I can't tell you how it's done, but there are ways. You walk into a shop, you know you've got to be at a certain place at a certain time and there is the book you need. If you're not in the right state of mind to do it, you can't do it. But if get into this mindset, you can...

KJ: Like dowsing?

IS: Very like dowsing.

KJ: What was the initial transition into book-dealing?

IS: Oh, total accident. In the early times, as I said, whenever I ran out of money I went down to Manpower or wherever to take what jobs were going, and do those and that was fine. But by the mid-seventies, that was running out, and I now had two small kids and was thinking, well, what's the next move to make, because we were finding it tough to survive. And by accident I got left some books by an old lady in Wales - not a vast lot, but they were quite nice. I kept a few that I was interested in for myself, and I took the rest round bookshops, and was astonished! People would either not even look at them, or would offer me a complete pittance, for things I knew the value of. So I thought, well, I'll try and sell them myself. There was a book market in Camden Passage, I took them out and whoosh! Tables disappeared, at our prices. And this began it. I thought, this is a feasible way of earning a living.... This was in about 1975, just after *Lud Heat* came out.

Up to the time of *White Chappell* it was my main income, and thereafter I was doing some dealing, some writing for quite a long time.

KJ: You've written so much about book-dealing, in various different formats, that I hardly feel I need to enquire any further; but tell me a little more about how it escalated from that one day on the stall.

IS: Well, once the stock I'd inherited began to run out, rapidly, I started locally, to search, and that got me into the Brick Lane/ Cheshire Street, Sunday morning market, which was astonishing at that time, an absolute eye-opener for me - getting down there at about five in the morning and seeing this entire blitzed landscape - which is now very developed, - covered with people selling everything: single shoes, warped records.. You really felt the cargoes of the world were falling through that place. And then Farringdon Road, representing the end of the Victorian era of book-dealing, when the whole street had been markets - it was an old Liberty, still there, with the eccentric George Jeffery operating his franchise, with amazing books coming out. Because he had the back-door entree to the big auction houses - they'd buy a country house library, cream it off and then give him the rest. It had fantastic stuff, because they always made a howler over what they took out.

So, plunging into that was the start, but in the end it wasn't enough, because we developed such a market that it required charging about, getting into all the country places, and luckily, fairly early on in this process, I took the decision to sell contemporary books. The market in Camden Passage was only on one side, and it only opened up on Fridays, and it was very much attached to the antiques trade, books as antiques - leather-bound books, all very elitist and slightly gay and a bit dreary. And I thought, well, you could sell contemporary books. So I persuaded the guy in charge, who was always looking for more income, to move to another site on the market and open on Thursdays, as a day just of books. So I sold modern first editions, as well as just interesting paperbacks, whatever you'd found, selling to the student-type characters as well as beginning to sell to the book trade.

And then on Brick Lane I met Martin Stone, who's this famous ex-rock musician, who was still playing a bit, and once he'd come in it all began to grow. John Baxter's new book, *A Pound of Paper* - I've just reviewed it for *The Independent* - describes this world, and is dedicated to Martin Stone. I think for a very brief time this book stall became the centre of civilization, because... what had happened was that the sixties people, a lot of the vanished, semi-destroyed figures, took their illusions and crept into this new, pre-Thatcherite Free Market world. It was like a parody of Thatcherism. There were left-overs from the sixties who had money, inheritances, trust funds, who wanted something a bit rock and roll, and dealing in modern first editions became that. So there were those characters, and then there were all those quasi-literary people, and then there was a nice middle-class element who sold to Americans...and private collectors who also sold on to other areas of the trade. They were all buying from the stall on Thursday morning. And it put on a phenomenal pressure to go out and turn up this stuff.

KJ: Hard work?

IS: It was fantastically hard work. You'd be down there at Thursday at roughly six o'clock in the morning, and would be there all day Thursday, and then all day Friday - on Friday I'd go to Portobello Road before going to Camden Passage, because that was a more relaxed day - the dealers would go on Thursday, and Friday was for the general public. So, Fridays, Portobello Road at six, then up to Camden Passage. Saturday morning I'd have to go to Farringdon Road, and then to Camden Passage, Sunday morning to Brick Lane by five o'clock... Monday was the only day I would have off. Tuesday, out on the road buying; Wednesday, prepare the stuff for Thursday. So that was it. Remorseless. Everything done on the hoof, a perpetual blur.

KJ: Which means no time to read; so that the education you speak of was mainly an oral education.

IS: Mostly, yeah. With Martin Stone and Driffield, it was reading on trains, because they didn't drive. But as I was driving, I couldn't read, except when I stopped at night. The other thing was that this whole culture of books became interwoven with the culture of cocaine, because a lot of those dealers were wired to the eyeballs, and of course they were making quite a lot of money, and dealing in cocaine as well... It was fascinating, a very, very un-described part of the culture which had a major influence. People like Mike Moorcock would be acquiring commodities from these dealers in exchange for his own typescripts and proofs, and the material gave him the energy to write books in three days... wonderful backwards-and-forwards lurches between different worlds, until you're into one of these Savile Row-type bookshops which look daunting to the outsider, and not realising that this grand operation is completely underwritten by these Dickensian low-lifes, plunging all over the map, pulling every stroke in the book.

KJ: Anyone who's worked in a bookshop knows that, if you're anything of a writer yourself, there's something deadening about always handling other people's work...

IS: There is, but this was unlike working in a bookshop. I spent days working in bookshops and found it absolutely soul-destroying, but this was perpetual movement. You arrive at, say, Hastings in the morning, and you are taking in the landscape... you go to the shops, but you're not blind, you take in the sea, the whole thing. And you'd be scribbling little things in notebooks... it wan't an endless, 24-hour a day focus on books, not with me, because the other thing still existed. At the back of my mind was the thought that at some point in all this I would stop and write this novel.

KJ: So what was the catalyst?

IS: I finally got the money. I got a couple of very good hits... bizarrely, I found a box of Ceri Richards - Lyre Birds which he had painted for the cover of *Poetry London*, and which had never been used. I kept one, sold the rest and that generated a few thousand quid. And also, Driffield was starting his magazine at that time, and he wanted to put a collection in front, so I put my Kerouac and Burroughs collection in, sold quite a lot of duplicates, things like proofs of *Naked Lunch*...this generated the money I needed and I took the time off. Also, Mike Goldmark had offered to publish the book, and said he'd give me some money for doing it as well. I should say here how grateful I am to Mike. His generosity changed my life. So the three things together gave me the time, and I wrote it in about six weeks, then took more time re-writing it. I really did need to do that book by that stage, it was now or never. If it hadn't worked, I don't know, I would have gone down some other route. But the book dealing thing was running out, I could see the writing on the wall for that. The free-lance, easy-going book trade was never going to last much longer, and was already moving into book fairs in hotels. The street thing was dead.. It was a period thing, absolutely a period thing. There's nothing like it now. A totally different set-up, though obviously some of the people who came into it at that time are still thriving by adapting.

KJ: I don't want to romanticise the importance of writing as an activity, but didn't you ever get the sense that being a book-dealer was a waste of time and talent?

IS: No, I didn't. I don't think of writing as being hermetically discrete from the rest of my life. What you do in your life is the primary thing, and this other activity works in and out of it, as it has done all along. It's only of late that I'm confronted with doing it as a way of making a living, having to come up with product... I don't really book deal at all any more. I occasionally, very occasionally, put a catalogue out, but there's nowhere for those catalogues to go any more, unless you go onto the Net.

KJ: I suppose I'm intrigued by the extent to which you seem to be immune to something that gnaws at almost every writer I know - the twin demons of feeling, self-laceratingly, horribly under-productive yourself, and at the same envious of certain other writers' productivity and wordly succcess. You don't seem to suffer from those worms. Why is that?

IS: I don't know why. [Laughs]. At that time, in the eighties, there was a surge of interest in contemporary fiction, and it became glamorous for a time - Rushdie, Barnes, Amis, all of that. And I manipulated that as a book-dealer, I could see that people were going to be collecting and dealing in what amounted to futures. So the books out this week were being traded up, whereas traditionally the second-hand book trade wouldn't touch anything that wasn't established. Even the thirties was a bit recent. So this stuff was anathema to them, but I thought it was a very good market to exploit. I didn't really think much of most of the writers - the fact that they were being successful didn't impinge on me in any way, because I didn't think I was operating in the same area at all.

The only point of crossover, I suppose, would have been Peter Ackroyd, and that was something of a stimulus in that he was able to take elements of *Lud Heat*, which was a completely obscure underground work, and parley it up into being a best-seller [*Hawksmoor*], which struck me as extraordinary, and did make me think, well, maybe I can punt this novel of mine in a way that would actually get it published by a proper publisher. Because I knew I couldn't afford to publish it myself, it was hopeless...

KJ: So did you hawk the manuscript around?

IS: Only in that Peter Ackroyd had said to me, in correspondence when he was doing *Hawksmoor*, that if I wrote a book he would give it to his publisher, who was Sinclair-Stevenson at that time. And the publisher looked at it and threw his hands up in horror, and didn't want anthing of it. And a girl that I sold quite a lot of books to was working as a secretary for [the editor at Jonathan Cape] Tom Maschler, and she knew that I was writing this thing and said, I'll show it to him. And he was sort of interested, but thought it was too strange... the reader at Cape recommended they should publish it, but Maschler said no. He sent me a letter saying, "When you've written your next one, do send it along"... But I knew Mike Goldmark would do it, or said he would do it, so I just went to him... I didn't want to waste time sending it to two dozen other publishers.

KJ: Although Goldmark had never published anything before, he made a very handsome job of it, which was one of the things that helped win it some favourable notice.

IS: That was his vision: to make a beautiful object. He spent a lot of time and money in getting it done right - by Mardersteig in Verona. But I don't think he even sent out review copies, but luckily a guy called Bill Webb, who was Literary Editor at *The Guardian*, took it up, wrote it up and nominated it for the *Guardian* fiction prize that year. At that point, the *Guardian* fiction prize was quite a grand thing, so suddenly, instead of going to the market on Thursday morning, I was going down to the *Guardian*'s prize-winning beano in a swanky Southwark, riverview apartment, where there was William Golding, and Salman Rushdie, and Angela Carter and Bill Webb said, "Who do you want to meet?" The Russian Cultural Ambassador was there, and they were all discussing [*White Chappell*] - they'd created it as an Official Runner-Up to a novel by Peter Benson called *The Levels*, which was a much more othordox novel, a bit like Graham Swift's *Waterland*, set in the Somerset levels... Bill Webb, I like to think, would have preferred *White Chappell*, he was fantastically supportive, got me some travelling scholarship money on the back of it. So, suddenly, this thing did have a certain presence, and was quite well reviewed in the broadsheets.. and Paladin bought it for paperback, thanks to Nick Austin, who was a very good editor, and had actually read an extract from it in Driff's magazine, and wanted to publish it even before Goldmark. So it would have come out, anyway, as a paperback original from Paladin.

KJ: When it had made its initial stir, though presumably no great fortune...

IS: [Laughs]

KJ: ...did you feel a sense of being slightly at a loss?

IS: No, no. I always plan about eight books ahead. It was in my head that there would be a quartet of books which would be to do with White Chapels of various sorts. The binding image of *White Chappell* itself is that there is this skeletal outline in the grass of this church, the original White Chapel of Whitechapel, a pilgrim church, in the park opposite the Whitechapel Gallery, where there's just a brick outline of a church... and there's a drinking fountain at the entrance of that church which says, "Dedicated to One Well Known and yet Unknown". That paradox, that ambiguity, haunted the whole project.

I'd plotted out all four books. *Landor's Tower* was going to be next, which would go back into the Welsh material, and notions of borderland. There was this particular chapel, where the novel as published finishes up, with the figure of Death on the wall and all of that. Also, in a sense, that novel would represent the West, as *White Chappell* represents the East. It was very Blakean, again. There was one plotted for the North, which I'm still working on. And a final one, which is in the South. Those two remain unwritten, but, as I say, I've plotted them. The Northern one is set in the Peak District, really... That was always the most obscure in my head, how that would work. I won't go into details.. Some of the same characters drift through, but largely it's thematic, and the secrets from the first book, *White Chappell*, are gradually worked through to a kind of revelation in the final one. The final one probably will be the Final One. And then the other books I've done in between times have just erupted out of the blue, for various programmatic reasons.

KJ: How do you look back on *White Chappell* now?

IS: I'm fond of it. I haven't re-read it, but for me it was obviously a major point in my life. It still belonged to that earlier era in lots of ways. And yet it predicts things that I wanted to do, in a looser way, ahead.

KJ: I've read it several times, and though a lot of the things about it which I initially found baffling now seem a lot more lucid, there are still plenty of things in it that escape me.

IS: The original sub-title was " A Book of Secrets", because the Ripper stuff was very dense and had been lived with for a long, long period of time, so in a sense you're getting a kind of ashy residue of a mountain of reading and learning and debate and discussion. There are actually three elements in the book - the present-tense, picaresque, knockabout of the book dealers, which you can get into as a narrative device; there's some very coded and probably obscure material to do with the Ripper, to do with speculations on history, including quite a lot of material from James Hinton and Gull - genuine letters, fragments of letters, re-worked letters, presented directly or otherwise; and then there's a third element, which is where the characters of Brian Catling and I, from an earlier period, working in breweries and so on, and carrying out the researches which deliver this material. And that third element is sort of lost. A

114

lot of people think of it as a tick-tock between Victorian Gothic and contemporary book-dealers running about, which it really isn't. There are always three things moving, always around and around this fixed point. If you think of it as a tilted topography..

The fictional element is a sleight-of-hand, really. It's a discussion, a debate about the nature of the pain and how it affected the landscape. It would need to be read more, I suppose, like a kind of poem, like a kind of *Waste Land* thing where there are references and echoes and quotes buried in it, and it's not going to reveal itself at one sitting. You can just slide through it with the book-dealers - and in a sense that's the history of my own intelligence up to that point. The book dealers represent the period we've just been talking about, this period of spinning about in a mad Thatcherite economy, but there are the ghosts of utopians and idealists of an earlier generation, labouring quietly in the landscape... and behind them all is this world where the large Victorian questions were debated and discussed, and where people came up with very eccentric solutions, that take you right back into the Egyptology we were talking about before.

KJ: Why, incidentally are "J" and "K" letters of ill omen in *White Chappell*? Bad news for me...

IS: For some reason, I was in a pub and just wrote down the initials of the [Ripper] victims, and they spell out this bizarre MANAC ES CEM, JK, which is like a dyslexic curse of some kind. I don't know, the J and K seemed to play across the landscape. One of the codings is that those initials keep coming back in different forms in terms of victims and sacrifices all the way through. There are a million possiblities - J.K. Husymans is one of them - but in that period of thinking in that way, and using these various systems of interpretation, backward reading, JK seemed to be a repeated device. And actually, the letter K is a vicious slash, just seeing it as calligraphy, a kind of wounding symbol, a brand.

KJ: And you're the victim today.

IS: ...OK.

KJ: When did your interest in the Ripper mythology begin?

IS: It was really more of an interest in place, in the Whitechapel ghetto, and if you are interested in that place and start to move about a bit, these crimes are horribly unappeased, and seem to dominate the territory. When I worked in the brewery, there was this old guy who was obsessed, had big glass plate studies that he'd taken of all the murder sites, and he seemed almost to have been a witness to the events and talked me through them, so I got all that. A lot of people were telling stories on the ground that fed into it, and the landscape of the place was not all that changed, in the early seventies, from the Victorian era. Apart from the bomb damage, you could actually see the structure of the thing, which is now horribly overlaid, but then wasn't. It was in a dozy limbo, where it had been forever.

★★★

PART FIVE:

DOWNRIVER TO *LONDON ORBITAL*
AND BEYOND

KJ: There's a period of, what, about five years between *White Chappell* and *Downriver....*

IS: Is there really? Yes, I guess so... I just dived back into book dealing. There was no money in *White Chappell*.

KJ: But it's very striking that, having produced lots of very small texts in the earlier years, your next major project is a thunderous great brick of a book.

IS: Well, I guess the advantage is that there *was* a gap. A chance to build up a head of steam and gather material, which is really my preferred way to work. If there were no financial considerations of any kind, I'd leave a decent gap between things, so that I'm drifting about, poking, doing slim things, fragments, and every so often erupt with some large tome that's been gathered over at least five or six years... but that indulgence is not possible any more. I think one of the reasons that *Downriver* worked quite well, was that there was this gap, and it had to be done with a real head of steam, because everything was becoming extremely difficult. Our house was being knocked about, because it was too small, bursting at the seams, so we had some serious building work done - washing up in the bath, then the bath disappeared, and I'm writing in clouds of brick dust... and then my father died in the middle of it, and I had to go backwards and forwards to Wales, and Anna went into hospital so I was looking after the children... It was the maddest, most difficult period of writing ever, but somehow that seemed to work in my favour.

KJ: All the stranger, then, that the book is so substantial.

IS: It was written at absolutely breakneck speed, in tiny gaps that I seized from all this chaos that was happening around me.

KJ: How long did it take?

IS: Not very long. Four or five months, really hammering away. That's why it has the form of these twelve separate pieces, because you could do one with great concentration, and then start another. It was more or less a fresh start each time.

KJ: *Downriver* is sometimes referred to as your Thatcher novel. Was that the intention?

IS: That wasn't how it started. I felt that in *White Chappell* I'd set out to appease these crimes, or deal with that in some way, but the whole focus of it ended up with paternalistic figures, wandering around enacting their various rituals and magics, and I wanted to do something that was loosely associated, the second time out, with something from the women. The first one I was going to do was the woman who was killed in Berners Street, Elizabeth Stride, who had always told this legend of being on the *Princess Alice* pleasure steamer which sank, and that her husband and children were drowned, but that she was pulled out of the river and given this second life, and then becomes a victim, years later, of Jack the Ripper. It's a very haunting theme.

And I still don't know why - because I knew that this ship had gone down near Woolwich - but for some reason I went out to

120

Tilbury first, and just walking into Tilbury, seeing that landscape, that whole down-river part of London, I realised that there were stories to be told. The story of the city really came out with the river. And the Ripper element of it, which is there in the first story, then disappears, although the appeasing of these ghosts is still an element throughout the book. And then as you come back towards London, it was the period when the whole Thatcherite explosion in Docklands was taking place, and the back-story was being eliminated in front of my eyes. Buildings disappearing overnight, huge principalities being thrown up, and it couldn't have been better for me... things were so bad they were really great to write about. So the two things mixed and met.

So the original version, the mythology I was working with, sort of slid underneath this superficial surface comedy and drama of the Thatcher thing, and the two interlinked.

KJ: Did the whole book come from London walking, or just the first section?

IS: It's called "A Grimoire of Rivers and Railways", and there was quite a lot of travelling about on these funny, dingy trains to the back end of nowhere. And then walking about. No epic walking - you'd go out to Tilbury, wander about for a day, in that area, or go to Woolwich. I didn't take off on huge walks from Hackney, though obviously I walked around the various zones and researched, in a loose way. Quite a lot of stuff was looked into with [the cultural historian] Patrick Wright, who was living in Dalston...

KJ: And becomes a character in the novel.

IS: Yes. He'd reviewed *White Chappell* for the *London Review of Books*, and started off with a huge spiel about Rodinsky's Room, which proved very fertile. And then we got into investigating that material ourselves, as fiction on my part, and he included his material in *A Journey Through Ruins*. So in some senses it was a mad poetic combined with journalistic investigation. We went together to Bow Quarter, this Bryant and May match-girls' factory that was being converted into flats for yuppies. Supposedly we were going to do a film as well. But his being there proved a useful fictional tool.

KJ: Why did the novel grow so large?

IS: That was its organic state. It needed to be that length...*White Chappell* was so boiled down... a residue, a glowing ash of something that had been cooked for a very long time, whereas *Downriver* was much fresher and looser. Like going into a world and seeing it rush away from you. There were epic forces at work, arguing over this landscape. It was freer and easier than *White Chappell*, which was pre-ordinated in quite a fixed form, like a series of rituals. It was a much more possessed book, which enacts itself like theatre, whereas *Downriver* doesn't, it's sort of slap-happy, wild cinema.

KJ: The reviews of the book were terrific - you only have to look at the paperback edition to see a great unanimous chorus of raves - but they were enthusiastic in a way that reads very strangely for anyone who actually knows you, even if only slightly. They make you out to be, well, a savage nutter...

IS: [Laughs] Well, I'm not responsible for the reviews. Reviews are always a weird reflection of what books actually are. Somebody generally sets a key note, and then everyone else grabs it and reflects it. Positive or negative, they don't very often connect up with how the books actually are. If you're going to get anything interesting written about them, they'll be in weird little magazines that come out of Cambridge or somewhere, where some strange student has a take which will say something. The newspaper reviews are pretty much meaningless, they're just the reflex responses of burned-out journalists. I know, because I now write them myself, and I don't stand by those very much, either.

KJ: But my question was not so much about the vagaries, the laziness or the cliche-mongering of journalists, but about what it is in a book like *Downriver* which creates that particular collective fantasy about what you are as a person.

IS: Well, I think if you take the middle-brow novel as the norm, then seeing these things portrayed, they look pretty manic and nutty and coming from somewhere else, an alien world. And the language itself is fairly savage, so it's uncomfortable. So you would assume that the person producing them is, equally, a kind of nutter.

KJ: Speaking of the language, I've noticed that there are strong premonitions of your characteristic prose style at least as early as *Kodak Mantra Diaries*, as though you're tapping into a rhythm, a range of vocabulary, a syntax which is quite spontaneous and natural to you, not something you'd contrived...

IS: Oh, no, no. No way. Just trying to get the most clear version of awkward thought processes. The rhythms that are natural to you. Sometimes very all-encompassing, sometimes very abrupt and stark. Changes of rhythm: bangbangbang bang.... drip... drip... drip. The equivalents of single-frame filming, or massive superimposition of organic film.

KJ: There's a very interesting passage in *Landor's Tower* where one of the characters gives vent to a kind of distilled version of all the bad notices you've ever had, or ever had nightmares about, and one of the things that he concentrates on is one of your trademark effects – a combination of abrupt groups of one, two or three words, with jagged syntactical fragments and a kind of sprightly running that doesn't always call on verbs...

IS: There was a period when the reviews started to focus entirely on the grammar, the syntax, and the linguistics of it - which is miles from my own head. But they couldn't deal with the matter of it. This thing, the technical language side of it, is natural to me, but also the only effective way for me to do this material. So you'd get people talking about the structure of paragraphs...

KJ:... which I assume is intuitive?

IS: Totally intuitive. It's evolved as a style. I'm now fairly comfortable with it, and can operate it quite quickly and smoothly.

KJ: Another thing that reviewers of *Downriver* were responding to was its splenetic side, its anger, though a lot of people at that time shared exactly the same sense of anger....

IS: I think so. I was trying to be funny - savagely funny - and not to simply get bogged down in rhetoric. Some of the satirical stuff is probably a bit clunky, I haven't re-read it. But nothing has changed, I still feel the same. You can make a passionate attack and still make it funny. The documentary books are not that different - *London Orbital* or whatever. In a way, it's already been rehearsed, because in *Radon Daughters* there's a Renchi character who accompanies the narrator on this walk to Oxford and Cambridge. And it's exactly a pre-vision of plodding around the M25. If you read that now, you'll see that it's already there in fictional form - and people found it unreadable. But if it's put into an apparently real landscape, they're quite happy to review it and discuss it - oh, here are these nutters walking around the M25, right. That seemed to be the switch that turned things round for me, and gained me some kind of audience: shifting out of fiction into non-fiction - or calling it non-fiction.

KJ: Not long after *Downriver* you curated your first really large exhibition, at the Goldmark Gallery, *The Shamanism of Intent...*

IS: I'd thought, in the same way that I'd thought at the time when we did the Albion Village show at the Whitechapel, that the moment had come round again, that we needed a show for all the people I wanted to write about - people like Gavin Jones, who was a fictional character in *Downriver* ... I just felt the moment was there for one of the exhibitions, and I couldn't possibly have approached the Whitechapel at that stage, so Goldmark agreed to hold it. I wanted an event, a three-dimensional event, that would take in painting with performance, readings, talks, the whole bit... and the sculpture of Steve Dilworth, who was one of the few people who got something out of the exhibition. He was living in the Hebrides, and his work was seldom seen in England.

KJ: He deserved to, his work is terrific... Was "Shamanism of Intent" just an eye-catching phrase, or was there something more to it?

IS: Well, no, there's always a serious edge... titles often arrive at the very last minute, but that was the blanket area that I was trying to pitch, the notion of some kind of possession or magic, outside the usual parameters. It wasn't an aesthetic or political movement..

KJ: Were most of the people in the show - Jones, Dilworth, Catling, Brian Lewis, Aaron Williamson and the others - already aware of each other, or were you the go-between, the introducer?

IS: I think there were connections - I'd met Steve through Brian Catling, originally - but on the whole, no.

KJ: Shamanism was a fairly hot topic in the sixties and early seventies..

IS: Well, everyone had read Castaneda [laughs]... The sense of Shamanism as a proper discipline, I think Catling would have been good at. He read about ethnographic material, he visited Africa, North Africa, which fed into some of the later collections of poems, so when he's talking about elements of ritual magic in those cultures, it's not wild man, magic mushroom stuff. It's someone who's spent a lot of time in museums and read books.

KJ: And I assume you must have read Mircea Eliade [i.e., his magisterial text *Shamanism: Archaic Techniques of Ecstasy*]

IS: Yes, yes, absolutely. So did Catling, I'm sure. He's also very keen on things like Eugene Marais, *The Soul of the White Ant...*

KJ: I've been trying in vain to get backing for a film about Marais...

IS: Oh, right.

KJ: How did *Radon Daughters* fit into the scheme of things? Once again, it's a digression from the master plan about the four white chapels.

IS: Nick Austin, my editor at Paladin, was always very keen on, obsessed by William Hope Hodgson, and wanted a sequel to *House on the Borderland*. He said, there's no money for *Downriver*, but I can get you this money for a sequel.. which then becomes *Radon Daughters*, but he's already out of that particular job by then, on to something else. Now, it's completely impossible to write a sequel to *The House on the Borderland*, because it ends with the death of the cosmos, time, and everything else, the recluse who's involved in this story is about to be devoured by alien beasts... there's nowhere to go, that's the whole point of it. A great, Wellsian fantasy, which I was always very fond of, but there's nothing you can do with it. So I was never really going to write a sequel, but I was interested in the figure of Hodgson and the way this story comes about, and having found, to my own satisfaction, the place where it was set - because it's quite reasonably described as to where it's set, so I went back to Ireland and found this place, the Burren, this fantastic landscape of limestone pavements lost in mist.

I was happy to go back to writing and carry on the political agenda of *Downriver*. *Downriver* is the Thatcherite book, and *Radon Daughters* belongs in the John Major era, it's really No Man's Land, there are no fixed political points, everything is very grey and pompous, everything's deeply depressed, and the only reality is this missing Gothic novel that's haunting the landscape, which is twinned with the business of the X-rays...

I saw these photographs in the London Hospital. The London Hospital was the only real archive of memory for Whitechapel, they had the best collection of images of the place, the best texts. I'd go into the basement of the London Hospital and see these very early X-ray photographs of hands with rings, and the people who took them - the flesh was rotting off them, they all died, they died of cancer. So the proposition is that there is a machine in the basement there which gives the narrator access to memory, and to the visionary world of Hodgson, but at the cost of destroying his own existence, which he knows. So it's a deranged proposition. But that was the metaphor for the business of writing it, as far as I was concerned. The business of dealing with these matters of London, saturating yourself with them, would mean that you were actually dooming yourself to fall apart - a Faustian pact. And that book is very grim, really, in lots of ways. I find it hard to read. It has a kind of manic comedy to it as well, but, again, it was sort of like *Suicide Bridge*, it became a dead end, and the culmination of that cycle...

KJ: And, like *Suicide Bridge*, it dips a toe into Cambridge.

IS: Yes... There's a triangulation between the lost Whitechapel Mound and the still-present mounds at Oxford and Cambridge. I believe the lost mound will come back again if I do this book I'm currently planning, this project of a great circular walk, sixty miles out from London. So you can see that things adapt into long-term projects.

Radon Daughters practically disappeared. It's strange, it's the most fictional of all my books in its form, and it's the favourite of people like William Gibson and Michael Moorcock and so on, certain writers, but it's absolutely unreadable to the general reader.

KJ: So, again, if *Radon Daughters* wasn't part of this East-West-North-South scheme...

IS: Yeah, once I'd finished it, I thought, now I can get on to *Landor's Tower*. So I went down to Wales, and there were all the things I mention in the novel - taking a cottage, finding it very haunted, and it turns out that it had belonged to Terry Waite, who's locked up in a Beirut cellar, and I can't write there, so I do the preliminary stuff and come back to London and get on with the next thing. Having to book-deal all the time, which was still my main living.

KJ: So when did you finally wean yourself from the trade?

IS: Probably not till *Lights Out for the Territory*. Because none of these books made any money - a pittance, which mixed with what I got from book-dealing, and journalism, and bits of TV and stuff was just enough to scratch by on. *Lights Out* was, to me, just a collection of bits and pieces which I'd written in between times, cannily re-vamped and given this walking structure and a psychogeographic make-over. It got very, very widely reviewed. Granta had not promoted it particularly, because their pitch, when they launched, was based on Jeanette Winterson and Nigel Williams, who were starry figures, in their way, from different areas. And mine was down at the bottom of the queue, but it hit some note, and started to sell quite rapidly. It always had the support of my Granta editor, Neil Belton. Fierce, intense, hair-trigger. Then there were loads and loads of follow-up schemes that took on the notion of psychogeography....

KJ: What do you think made it such a hit?

IS: I don't know, it was quite astonishing. I think, in a sense, all the other stuff had remained resolutely underground. All these themes had been rehearsed, and then a lot of those bits which appeared in *Lights Out* had had a pre-run in places like *London Review of Books* and were half-lodged in some people's minds. Also I think it came at the right time politically, at a moment when people wanted those things said about the Thatcherite era and the disasters that had been created for London. And so, accidentally, because it belonged to an earlier era, it came at the right time. Most of what I do comes at the wrong time - either several years before people come to a consensus of this kind, or so out of date and oblique and lost that it's never going to find a consensus. But that one, just by sheer accident... I mean, it was reviewed by the likes of Ken Livingstone, favourably, and Dianne Abbot, political figures, saying comfortable things about the corruptions that were there before them. And also, somehow, if you do numbers about London and its mysteries, it's always relatively popular - that Ackroydian area.

KJ: One of the things I enjoy and admire about the book is the way you used it to celebrate and promote a whole range of marginal and neglected artists and writers - some people I knew a little about and wanted to know more, and some people I'd never heard of, but was delighted to know about...

IS: Most of these figures had always been presences in the fiction, and no one wanted to know about them as they were in their Blakean emanations. People like Brian Catling, who I write about in a parodic version in the novels as Joblard. The whole cinema business with Tom Baker and Mike Reeves is tucked away in various poems... I think it was handy actually to spell it out, and to pay credit, because I think the culture is infinitely lazy at the moment. There are now books being written about Mike Reeves...

Patrick Keiller, who was also being written about quite a lot at the time that the book came, was on the same button with his film *London* as I was with *Lights Out*. It got very widely reviewed and covered and promoted in a way that the subsequent one [*Robinson in Space*] didn't. Because once you go back to the same territory, people are never as easy... I thought very substantial people were just going undiscussed.

KJ: You're not kidding...

[*There followed a long, bitter, partisan and at times probably libellous discussion on the contemporary culture of ignorance. When feelings had calmed a little, the interview resumed:*]

KJ: Tell me about the origins of *Slow Chocolate Autopsy.*

IS: Oh, that was a fairly throwaway project, it was just that I wanted to collaborate with Dave McKean, whom I'd met at a science-fiction convention years ago. We'd talked of doing things together, his designs are quite in tune with the way I write, so we assembled, quite rapidly, a series of texts, some photographic elements that were a bit like film scripts or story-boards. A nice-looking book, but the material is, I guess, fairly light and instant.

KJ: But it was also an experiment with a new alter ego figure, Norton.

IS: There was a notion of being trapped by the hackdom of writing, being trapped into having to write about the city, so it was a lightweight comment on the situation I'd written myself into at that time, as being defined as a person who could only write about London. Certainly, when I wrote the one book about Wales [*Landor's Tower*], there was a real antipathy towards it, as being an illegitimate production. Nobody wanted to know - get back, you have to write about London, that's what you do. And Norton had a sense of frustration - he keeps trying to escape the temporal and spatial limitations of the city and is thrown back every time. He's a sort of eternal hack, through various periods of time and history.

KJ: One of the things that you've obviously been able to do, subsequent to the success of *Lights Out*, is to make a return to film-making on a more public scale, with your Chris Petit collaborations - *The Falconer, Asylum, London Orbital*...

IS: That's been very nice. The real thing there was that the technology made it suddenly feasible again. Using little DV cameras was exactly like using the old 8mm Bolexes, and you could actually re-run the 8mm footage and interrogate it on screen without any hassle. When Chris Petit and I did the editing on our first collaboration, *The Cardinal and the Corpse*, the editing was so slow and clunky, even though it was on tape, that you just sat there for hours and hours... and now, with *London Orbital*, it's back to the freedom of writing you had back in the sixties, with home publishing, except that by accident Channel 4 are giving you sponsorship. It's been treated quite well - as a rather unusual documentary form, but really it's not that unusual at all, it's just what I was filming in the sixties. [Laughs]

KJ: So there's been something like a three-decade hiccup in your film-making career - you began there, and now you're back there again.

IS: Yeah. But now, though it's very nice to be able to do it, it's a secondary activity. I don't have any ambition to be permanently employed as a film-maker, but it's great, in parallel with a written project, to have a film project that takes you into different areas. Film, basically, is about driving, having done the walk. Doing the film of *London Orbital* doubled up the information base I had to draw on in the writng the book.

KJ: Do you see there being more films of a kind that are not necessarily tied in with a book project? I mean, *The Falconer* is only very loosely tied in with *Slow Chocolate Autopsy*...

IS: Well, one of the stories in that book is about Peter Whitehead having a heart attack, and you have lots of falcons and Egypt... *The Falconer* is very like a graphic novel - Dave McKean was involved in the film, and there were *Batman* women appearing, all of that.

KJ: Has Whitehead been in touch since...?

IS: Since the debacle over *The Falconer*? No. He's disappeared. Initially he loved the film. Originally the film wasn't meant to be about him, but his determination to tell his story was such that he kept bombarding us with amazing fragments and endless images, because he's one of the few people whose entire life was documented in images, right back to the sixties. Our paths crossed for the first time in the sixties - the sound man I had on *Kodak Mantra Diaries* came from his offices, which I visited, in Soho... He was living in a house which was full of masks and strange birds and things. Obviously he was doing his own Ginsberg film at the Albert Hall, *Wholly Communion*. Which was another story.

KJ: I think the dodgiest item I have in my entire book collection is a specimen called *Baby Doll*, by Peter Whitehead, which I unwittingly acquired from a catalogue which said it had an introduction by a certain Iain Sinclair.

IS: Oh my God!...[Laughs] There's a film loosely based on that called *Daddy*. A nightmarish film. Made with Nikki de Saint-Phalle, and shot in some chateau in France... unspeakable. Curiously enough, Chris Petit gets to review it in the *Time Out Film Guide*. But because I was caught up with Whitehead at that time, I produced this piece of text... I couldn't even bring myself to look at the material in the book [soft-core porn shots of a teenage girl], so it was done without even seeing it... I did it within the mode of *Slow Chocolate Autopsy*, treating all this as a fictional character doing this quite strange stuff.

KJ: And you re-ran this piece of *Baby Doll* prose-poetry in one of your small books of poetry, *The Ebbing of the Kraft*.

IS: Yeah.

KJ: What's the photograph on the cover of that book - a group of people on a boat?

IS: It's my photograph - in my mind, it's like Bergman's *Hour of the Wolf*, you know that boat scene? Apocalyptic... one of those voyages. A voyage down the Thames, where it's beginning to go out into the North Sea, and things are getting seriously spooky.... there's Brian Catling, and the photographer Francoise Lacroix, who's Marc Atkins' partner, and another woman who somehow just got herself onto the boat - and here we are, all shooting off into the sea. This would have been just before we were making *The Falconer*. Paul Burwell, who's a musician, with Bow Gamelan, is also a trained river-boat man, he went to the Royal Nautical School, and he had an old boat and took us on this voyage to Southend, a two-day voyage, and ended up trying to sail across to one of those off-shore forts. And the sea began to get really rough, Marc was incredibly ill, puking under a tarpaulin in a corner... Petit had take to his bed, because he had some kind of horror fantasy of being trapped on the river anyway, so these were the only ones left standing when I took the photo.

KJ: *London Orbital* is something that in one sense I know far too much about, having bled in the course of its making... but take me back to its origins, anyway.

IS: It was really very simple. To sum it up: I set out in the early days to write poetry, to publish and be in control of my own books, do loosely associated essay material to do with the city and speculations about all kinds without ever really having to interest other people in it. But once I got into the writing of fiction, then I was living the double life of book-dealing and producing fiction. And, by the early nineties I suppose, I thought of myself as a writer of fiction, but really there was no way of making a living at it and it was quite evident that this was coming to a dead end. So, strategically, I thought, if I re-present very much the same material as non-fiction, it'll probably do a lot better. So I took a chunk of London essays and tried to clarify what I was doing in a way that people could follow a bit better, and the result, *Lights Out for the Territory,* was pretty successful, for the first time, in a way my fiction had not been. So having done a lot about, particularly, the East End, the river, certain elements of Westminster and Jeffrey Archer, then really the next territory you have to go to is on the fringes, which to me were getting more interesting - I think the whole move is out there now, particularly towards Thames Gateway and the retail villages and... the disappearance of the old Victorian asylums, which is like the disappearance of Victorian Gothic literature.

KJ: Can you remember the germ of the idea of doing it as a continuous, counter-clockwise walk around the M25?

IS: Everything I did was always based on walking, so having decided that the M25 more or less described this perimeter fence of London, then the only way to deal with it from my point of view was to walk it. No use driving around it - if you do that, there's nothing but the drive. Having gone out to Waltham Abbey, and poked about there, I thought, this road *is* the river, the M25 is the equivalent of the Thames...

KJ: And was Waltham Abbey a spin-off from the Rodinksy researches?

IS: No, no, the reason was really that I'd always enjoyed walking up the Lea Valley, the Lea Valley represents zero longitude, so exorcism of the Dome stirred everything up...

I mean, all the time, really from *Downriver*, any London writers or visionaries of whatever stripe have to counter the main political culture. Because Thatcher introduced occultism into British political life..

KJ: Explain yourself, sir.

IS: Her take, if you look at it, verges on the demonic. She wanted to physically remake, she wanted to destroy the power of London, the mob, all of those things, which finally through the Poll Tax riots brought her down. I can't look at it in any other way but as actual demonic possession. She opened herself up to the darkest demons of world politics, and therefore writers were obliged to counter this by equally extraordinary projects. The whole notion of *Downriver* was an anti-demonic project, and this one, *London Orbital*, is against the New Labour project as it stands, with the symbol of the road repeating the symbol of the Dome. Two Circles. So you have to start with the Dome, head up zero longitude, and then you hit the M25 at Waltham Abbey. Waltham Abbey is the Cathedral of the

Road, King Harold is buried there, there's every reason to start there. And then off you go, counter-clockwise, very simple. And soon you move into H.G. Wells and *The War of the Worlds*, you move round to Ballard, you move through Bram Stoker - there are large imaginative projects which take place around this structure of London. So there it was, a book that just invited itself to be written. The easiest one I've ever done. The only one that's got a form, a beginning and an end.

KJ: You've now been in an extremely, even a dauntingly prolific phase for about a decade now; are you going to be able to take a pause now that the whole M25 project is tucked away, and let yourself reconsider, plan, rest?

IS: [Laughs]

KJ: I take it that means no?

IS: It's worse now. The M25 obviously ends another cycle, follow-ing on from *Lights Out*, and now, with this toe-hold on the South Coast [the flat in Hastings], I can see another era kicking in, which I hope will lead to doing this long journey I just mentioned, in a circle 60 miles from London... because all of these places along the coast here reflect London, they are part of London - the dispersed of Hackney and Tottenham are down here, the asylum seekers... amazing stuff is going on, exactly like Hackney in the sixties. And along the coast you have Derek Jarman's hutch, Dungeness, Margate... great ghosts of the culture all the way along the coast.

The working title for the project is *Sixty Miles Out*, based on Ford Madox Ford's 1909 vision of the future of London, where you set a compass point in Threadneedle Street, and make a sixty-mile circle, and all of that is London, in his mind. He has a very good take on that, which I quote in *London Orbital*. I think that's where to go now - follow the coast round, cut up through Cambridge and back down through Oxford, and swoop around, walk that circuit, see what's out there on the rim of where London really loses its identity. Because if you follow, say, Renchi - who's moved out to Glastonbury - London is not in any way part of your horizon. But if you're in Hastings or Margate or Broadstairs, you're still basically pitched back towards London. So I'd like to explore that ultimate boundary, as the final book in the series.

That's the long-term project, but there are subsidiary ones that have to be cranked out to keep the thing going. I've mentioned the white chapel sequence of four books, and I still want to do the remaining two. More locally, I'm going to something which is part documentary, part fiction, set on the coast, and the A13 journey out of London towards the coast - the kind of Dagenham, Ford Motor Company, Rainham Marshes, grungy journey out of London towards an aspirational coast. Then there's a John Clare project - based on John Clare's walk from Epping Forest back to his home. I've done the walk, written notes, taken lots of photographs - it's not written up.

The A13 book - it soon became obvious that Joseph Conrad enters the story. Conrad, coming back from the Congo after gathering the material which became *Heart of Darkness,* has a complete mental and physical breakdown and ends up in the German Hospital, which is just 300 yards up the road from where I live in Hackney. So the initial earthing in English soil of *Heart of Darkness* is just 300 yards away. And the second place Conrad lived in England was in Stoke Newington. Close to the street where Jack the Hat was murdered. So the Heart of Darkness is all there! You just stumble on these things by accident...

[*There followed a long digression on the pleasures of chance discovery, and the Situationist idea of the "derive", or drift.*]

KJ: And you once mentioned the possibility of a non-fiction book on the Beats?

IS: It's there, somewhere, though I don't know where it will fit in. I'd like to re-incorporate *Kodak Mantra Diaries* into it, because that's never been reprinted. There's the film script with Burroughs - and then there's material from a journey I made through America for a BBC radio programme a few years ago, where I had the chance to interview all these now very venerable Beats, with their bizarre takes on who was important in England, like P.G. Wodehouse, Evelyn Waugh, Peter Ackroyd. They had no interest at all in anything avant-garde or cutting-edge.

KJ: You've said that your life has now moved from one in which writing was one activity among others to one in which it's basically your profession. How does that feel?

IS: It feels OK... but it's more difficult, because in the early days there was a double identity. The writing was secret, I felt really in control of it, and it didn't matter whether it came through or not, I didn't have to produce because I did this other thing to earn a living, which took up a lot of time but gave me material to write about. Now the writing is there, that's it, it's the primary activity, and there's also an enormous sense of people looking over your shoulder, to see what you're doing. It's more difficult, because I can't just reel off in any direction, it's got to have some possibility of being punted in the market-place. And although I'll do little off-shoot projects for nothing, for private presses, I have to come through with the goods every two or three books. It's like making movies - three disasters on the trot and that's it. It's a tough environment. And I would then be completely cut loose, and back to selling books. So there's a fall-back position - I've got a lot of books on the shelves, so if it all goes seriously belly-up, I'll go back to being a book dealer.

KJ: If you were completely freed from economic necessity - say, if a juicy American grant came through - would it change the way you write?

138

IS: Not at all. Exactly the same. I might get lazy, I'm sure I would, and not do journalism, reviews or whatever, but the other stuff wouldn't change in any way. I'm not writing it because I believe I can sell loads of copies, I don't, it just isn't going to happen.

KJ: Now that, relatively speaking, you're famous, do you have any sense of your power as a sponsor or patron of other writers and artists?

IS: Oh, it's minimal... Looking back on that poetry world of the sixties and early seventies that we were talking about, it's quite interesting to think about what it was and what it's become subsequently. Because it's a world that no longer exists, in that there was a fairly real audience for it, there were a lot of publications, magazines that did these interviews at length with various poets, they inter-acted, and the world at large was at one remove, didn't need to impinge on this. With the harsh passage of time, some of those characters have survived in various ways: Brian Catling is a Professor at the Ruskin School of Fine Art in Oxford, Allen Fisher has been made a professor, Bill Griffiths is Dr. Griffiths, though he's still obviously not in a state of economic ease, he has to work very hard... Barry McSweeney died. These differences between trying to find a public audience and trying to find a way to operate in his own life... it just wasn't working out. He drank himself to death, basically. Wanting an audience, which another culture would have given him, because he was initally a very glamorous, youthful poet. But, finally, he was disregarded. When his books were published by Paladin, they were just pulped and dumped... which was a blow.

KJ: A final question. If some angry psychotic, like Bill Drummond's ex-squaddie pal Gimpo, came bursting through your door and blew you up with a grenade, what would you want on your tombstone?

IS: "You Bugger!" [Laughs]

KJ: No, come on...

IS: I don't want any tombstone. I really don't, I just want to disappear when the time comes. There's a tombstone up above us, on the hill, this absurd pyramid that's been made for the founder of St Leonard's, this guy James Burton. A curious pyramid with letter-box slits, that you can climb up to and peek into, rather in the way that you can see into [Richard] Burton's tomb in Mortlake - Black Burton, the explorer, who wanted to be left in a tent in the desert, and his wife erects this stone tent which is compeletely fixed in London suburbia. So anyone who has plans as to where they should stand or what their ultimate fate is can forget it. Best just to be turned into ash and blown to the four winds.

IAIN SINCLAIR: A SELECT BIBLIOGRAPHY

This list, as complete as I have been able to make it with limited resources, is meant to cover all of Iain Sinclair's principal publications from 1970 to 2002; it does not, that is, include prefaces, introductions, anthologies (except those edited by Sinclair), essays, reviews or journalism. Otherwise, it's pretty reliable. KJ.

Back Garden Poems. Albion Village Press, 1970. Illustrations by Lawrence ("Renchi") Bicknell. Poems. Edition of about 100 copies.

The Kodak Mantra Diaries. Albion Village Press, 1971. Photographs by the author, Anna Sinclair, Andrew Whittuck, Robert Klinkert. Unusual format (15" x 5 1/2"), card covers and spiral bound. Prose documentary about Allen Ginsberg and the "Dialectics of Liberation" conference, including interview transcripts, poems, letters and fragments. 2,000 copies.

Muscat's Würm. Albion Village Press, 1972. Illustrations and photograph of author by "William Gull", i.e. Brian Catling. Poems. 100 copies.

The Birth Rug. Albion Village Press, 1973. Photographs by author, "light plates" by Renchi Bicknell. Poems. 200 copies.

Groucho Positive/Groucho Negative. The Village Press, King's Road 1973. Essay on the Marx Brother. Wrappers. 200 copies.

Lud Heat. Albion Village Press, 1975. Photographs by author, maps by Brian Catling, yellow wrappers with tipped-in Hablot Browne engravings. Poems, prose poems and essays. 400 copies. Plus 10 casebound copies, in black cloth with additional holograph material.

Lud Heat. The English Language Society/The Lewis-Graham Press, 1986. Facsimile of first edition. 100 copies.

Lud Heat. Goldmark, 1987. Black boards, yellow dust-wrapper, engraving printed in white. 250 copies, of which 25 numbered and signed, with additional holograph material.

Lud Heat/Suicide Bridge. Vintage, 1995. Cover photograph by Marc Atkins. With an introduction by Michael Moorcock. Subsequent paperback editions by Granta.

Brown Clouds. Pig Press, 1977. Poems. 200 copies.

The Penances. The Many Press, 1977. Poems. Illustrated by Donal Ryan. 200 copies.

Bladud of Bath. Albion Village Press, c. 1978. An early version of some *Suicide Bridge* material. Illustrated by Donal Ryan; single folded sheet, issued gratis by Compendium Bookshop. About 100 copies.

Suicide Bridge. Albion Village Press, 1979. Photographs by author. Drawings by Susan Wood. Poems and essays. 400 copies, plus 15 casebound, signed and numbered, with additional holograph material.

Fluxions. Albion Drive Chapbook, 1983. Tipped-in postcard of "City of Lincoln". Green card wrappers, spiral bound. Poems. 21 copies, of which 14 were given away.

Flesh Eggs and Scalp Metal. Hoarse Commerce, 1983. [Not to be confused with the later Paladin collection of the same title.] Grey wrappers, white label, tracing-paper dust-wrapper. Poems. 12 numbered copies, given away.

Autistic Poses. Hors commerce, 1985. Orange wrappers, spiral bound, colour xerox of linocut by William Sinclair. Poems. 10 numbered copies, plus 1 for Mike Goldmark.

White Chappell, Scarlet Tracings. Goldmark, 1987. Frontispiece by Rigby Graham. Novel. 2000 copies of hardcover trade edition on Bodonia paper; limited edition of 100, numbered, on mould-made paper, with an original etching by Rigby Graham; 26 copies, lettered A to Z, *hors commerce*, with an aquatint by Rigby Graham and holograph material by the author.

White Chappell, Scarlet Tracings. Paladin, 1988, 1991 (2nd printing). Paper-back, with cover illustration by Richard Parent.

White Chappell, Scarlet Tracings. Vintage, 1995. Subsequent paperback editions from Granta.

Significant Wreckage. Words Press, 1988. Poems. Green wrappers, stapled. 200 copies, of which 75 signed and numbered by the author.

Flesh Eggs and Scalp Metal: Selected Poems 1970-1987. Paladin, 1989. Paper-back. Cover by Richard Parent.

Downriver, Or, The Vessels of Wrath. Paladin Grafton, 1991. Hardback, with archive illustrations. Dust wrapper shows "Apocalyptic Landscape" by Ludwig Meidner. Novel.

Downriver, Or, The Vessels of Wrath. Vintage, 1995. Paperback. Subsequent paperback editions from Granta.

Downriver (Or, The Vessels of Wrath). A Narrative in Twelve Tales. Random House. New York 1993. In American edition, revised. With new introduction by author. Jacket photograph by the Douglas Brothers.

The Shamanism of Intent: Some Flights of Redemption. Goldmark, 1991. Catalogue of the exhibition curated by Sinclair at the Goldmark Gallery, Uppingham 20 July - 24 August 1991. Many photographs and reproduction of artists' works.

Jack Elam's Other Eye. Hoarse Commerz, 1991. Poems. 200 copies.

Radon Daughters. Jonathan Cape, 1994. Hardback; cover photograph by Marc Atkins. Novel.

Radon Daughters. Vintage, 1995. Subsequent paperback from Granta.

Conductors of Chaos: A Poetry Anthology. Picador, 1996. Paperback original.

Penguin Modern Poets 10.1996 With Denise Riley, Douglas Oliver. Paperback original.

Lights Out for the Territory. Granta, 1997. Large format paperback. Photographs (including montage of London cityscape on covers and author's portrait) and drawings by Marc Atkins. Essays and reportage.

Lights Out for the Territory. Goldmark, 1997. 250 numbered, cloth bound, hard back copies in slipcase signed by author and photographer. With an additional 26 copies, lettered A-Z with additional holograph material & signed original print. And a further 15 *hors commerce* copies, numbered.

Lights Out for the Territory. Granta 1998. Paperback. With glossy photographs by Marc Atkins (a slightly different selection) bound in to the centre of the volume rather than printed directly on to the page, and an index.

The Ebbing of the Kraft. Equipage, 1997. Yellow board, stapled, cover photograph by the author. Poems.

Slow Chocolate Autopsy. Phoenix House,1997. Designs and illustrations by Dave McKean. Short stories. Hardback.

Slow Chocolate Autopsy. Phoenix House, 1997. Slipcased edition, purple cloth, limited to 200 numbered copies, signed by author and illustrator.

143

Slow Chocolate Autopsy. Phoenix House, 1998. Paperback.

Liquid City. Reaktion, 1999. A collection of photographs by Marc Atkins, many taken during the *Lights Out for the Territory* London walks, with a series of short accompanying essays, poems and anecdotes by Sinclair.

Rodinsky's Room (with Rachel Lichtenstein), Granta, 1999. Many photographs, reproductions of ephemera, illustrations. Essays on the enigma of David Rodinsky.

Rodinsky's Room. Goldmark, 1999. 250 numbered, clothbound, hardback copies in slipcase; signed by author. An additional 26 copies are lettered A-Z and contains an extra photograph and holographic material. A further 15 hors commerce copies are numbered I- XV.

Crash. British Film Institute, 1999. Critical monograph in the "Modern Classics" series. Many stills from David Cronenberg's film, as well as production stills and other archival images.

Dark Lanthorns: Rodinsky as Psychogeographer, Goldmark, 1999. Photographs by the author. Essays supplementary to *Rodinsky's Room.*

Sorry Meniscus (Excursions to tthe Millennium Dome). Profile Books, 1999. Reportage and polemic against the Millennium Dome.

Landor's Tower. Granta, 2001. Novel. Cover and illustrations by Dave McKean.

Landor's Tower. Goldmark, 2001. 250 numbered clothbound, hardback copies in slipcases; signed by author and illustrator. An additional 26 copies are lettered A-Z and contain holographic material. There are a further 15 hors commerce copies numbered I-XV.

Walking up Walls. Agnew's, 2001. Text to accompany concertina of Jock McFadyen postcards.

London Orbital. Granta, 2002. Essays and reportage. Cover by Dave McKean, colour plates by Dave McKean from photographs by the author, illustrations by Renchi Bicknell.

London Orbital. Goldmark, 2002. Limited edition, in slip cover, with additional chapter and holographic material.

Saddling the Rabbit. Etruscan Books, 2002. Poems. Wrappers.

Saddling the Rabbit. Etruscan Books, 2002. 26 copies cased and lettered A-Z, with additional holographic material. 26 copies cased, numbered and signed. 15 numbered copies *hors commerce*.

White Goods. Goldmark, 2002. Prose pieces, supplementary to *London Orbital*. 250 hardback copies: of which the first 100 are numbered and signed by author and artist. An additional 26 specially bound copies are lettered A-Z and signed, and contain holographic material. 15 copies hors commerce numbered I-XV.

Poets' Poems No.9. Aggie Weston's Editions, 2002. A selection of poems with some bearing on *Landor's Tower*, including the work of Henry Vaughan, David Jones, Chris Torrance, Ed Dorn, J.H. Prynne, Brian Catling, Vernon Watkins, W.S. Landor.

INDEX OF PHOTOGRAPHS

All photographs and ephemera are from the estate of Iain Sinclair.

Worple Press is an independent publishing house that specialises in poetry, art and alternative titles. *Worple Press* can be contacted at:
PO Box 328, Tonbridge, Kent TN9 1WR Tel 01732 368 958
email: theworpleco@aol.com
Trade orders: Central Books, 99 Wallis Road, London E9 5LN
Tel 0845 4589911

Titles Include:

Sailing to Hokkaido – Joseph Woods
(A5 Price £6.00 ISBN 0 9530947-6-6, pp 60)
Winner of the Patrick Kavanagh Award for Best First Collection

'If Woods is technically expert it is not to dazzle but to reveal his subject matter... his work as a whole shows an impressive reach and range'
Eiléan Ní Chuilleanáin

The Falls – Clive Wilmer
(A5 Price £6.00 ISBN 0 9530947-3-1, pp. 48)

'Boldly lyrical, broad in reference, felicitous in the craft of verse'
Elizabeth Jennings

Choosing an England – Peter Carpenter
(A5 Price £5.95 ISBN 0 9530947-0-7, pp. 48)

'Honest, considered and moving... Peter Carpenter has tied some new marriage knot around post-modernist and mainstream verse...'
David Morley

A Ruskin Alphabet - Kevin Jackson
(A6 Price £4.50 ISBN 0 9530947-2-3, pp. 88)

'You may like to consult *A Ruskin Alphabet* by Kevin Jackson, a collection of facts about and opinions on Ruskin and Ruskinites, together with a variety of pithy remarks from the man himself...'
Jim Campbell TLS

Looking In All Directions – Peter Kane Dufault
(A5 Price £10.00 ISBN 0 9530947-5-8, pp. 188)

'He observes the physical world keenly, and idiosyncratically, and frequently serves the "didactic muse", but he can sing from the heart too. Even at his most personal he is reaching for something fundamental about the relationship between man and nature. It is surprising that other publishers have ignored Dufault; but Worple Press have done him proud'

John Greening TLS

'Wonderful stuff'

Ted Hughes

Of Science – David Morley & Andy Brown
(A5 Price £6.00 ISBN 0 9530947-4-X, pp. 48)

'A well put together selection of poems, that moves from birds through trees, sea, ice, cities...'

Jane Routh

The Great Friend and Other Translated Poems – Peter Robinson
(A5 Price £8.00 ISBN 0-9530947-7-4, pp. 75)

Poetry Book Society Recommended Translation
'I was delighted by some of the poems. A good snapshot of the work of some fine writers, translated, it seemed to me, with sensitivity and respect.'

Catherine Smith

Nowhere Better Than This – Anthony Wilson
(A5 Price £9.00 ISBN 0-9530947-8-2, pp. 85)

'Anthony Wilson's work is shaped by both wit and compassion.'

Mark Robinson